SADE / FOURIER / LOYOLA

ALSO BY ROLAND BARTHES

On Racine

Writing Degree Zero

Elements of Semiology

Mythologies

S/Z

The Pleasure of the Text

SADE

FOURIER

LOYOLA

ROLAND BARTHES

Translated by Richard Miller

University of California Press
BERKELEY AND LOS ANGELES

University of California Press
Berkeley and Los Angeles
First California Paperback Printing 1989
Published by Agreement with Farrar, Straus and Giroux, Inc.
Translation © 1976 by Farrar, Straus and Giroux, Inc.
Originally published in French as *Sade, Fourier, Loyola*
© 1971 by Éditions du Seuil, Paris
First American edition, 1976
Printed in the United States of America
Designed by Charles E. Skaggs
1 2 3 4 5 6 7 8 9 10
Library of Congress Cataloging-in-Publication Data
Barthes, Roland.
Sade, Fourier, Loyola.

Translation of: Sade, Fourier, Loyola.
Includes bibliographical references.
1. Sade, marquis de, 1740-1814--
Criticism and interpretation.
2. Fourier, Charles, 1772-1837.
3. Ignatius, of Loyola, Saint, 1491-1556. I. Title.
PQ2063.S3B313   1989   808   88-29580
ISBN 0-520-06628-6 (alk. paper)

Contents

SADE / FOURIER / LOYOLA

Preface

From sade to fourier, sadism is lost; from Loyola to Sade, divine interlocution. Otherwise, the same writing: the same sensual pleasure in classification, the same mania for cutting up (the body of Christ, the body of the victim, the human soul), the same enumerative obsession (accounting for sins, tortures, passions, and even for accounting errors), the same image practice (imitation, tableau, séance), the same erotic, fantasmatic fashioning of the social system. None of these three authors is bearable; each makes pleasure, happiness, communication dependent on an inflexible order or, to be even more offensive, a combinative. Here they are all three brought together, the evil writer, the great utopian, and the Jesuit saint. There is no intentional provocation in this assembling (were there provocation, it would rather consist in treating Sade, Fourier, and Loyola as though they had not had faith: in God, the Future, Nature), no transcendence (the sadist, the contestator, and the mystic are not redeemed by sadism, revolution, religion), and, I add (which is the meaning of this preface), no arbitrariness: each of these studies, although first published (in part) separately, was from the first conceived to join the others in one book: the book of Logothetes, founders of languages.

The language they found is obviously not linguistic, a language of communication. It is a new language, traversed by (or traversing) natural language, but open only to the semiological definition of Text. That does not prevent this artificial language (perhaps because here it is supported by ancient

3

authors, caught in a two-part classical structure, that of representation and of style, a twofold trap from which modern output from Lautréamont to Guyotat has struggled to escape) from partially following the constituent paths of the natural language; and in their activities as logothetes, our authors, it seems, have each had recourse to the same operations.

The first is self-isolation. The new language must arise from a material vacuum; an anterior space must separate it from the other common, idle, outmoded language, whose "noise" might hinder it: no interference of signs; in elaborating the language in which the exercitant can interrogate the Divinity, Loyola requires retreat: no sound, little light, solitude; Sade shuts his libertines up in inviolable places (the Château of Silling, the convent of Sainte-Marie-des-Bois); Fourier decrees the dispersal of libraries, six hundred thousand volumes of philosophy, economy, ethics, censured, flouted, fit for distracting children (similarly Sade, leading Juliette and Clairwil into the cell of Claude the Carmelite, disdainfully draws the line at all the erotic forerunners that form the monk's worldly library).

The second operation is articulation. No languages without distinct signs. Fourier divides mankind into 1,620 fixed passions, combinable but not transformable; Sade distributes ejaculation like the words in a sentence (postures, figures, episodes, séances); Loyola cuts up the body (successively experienced by each of the five senses) as he cuts up the Christian narrative (divided into "mysteries" in the theatrical meaning of the word). Nor any language unless these cut-up signs are reprised in a combinative; our three authors deduct, combine, arrange, endlessly produce rules of assemblage; they substitute syntax, *composition* (a rhetorical, Ignatian word) for creation; all three fetishists, devoted to the cut-up body, for them the reconstitution of a whole can be no more than a summation of intelligibles: nothing indecipherable, no irreducible quality of ejaculation, happiness, communication: nothing is that is not spoken: for Sade and for Fourier, Eros and Psyche must be *articulated,* just as for Bossuet (defending Ignatius against the mystics of the ineffable, St. John of the Cross and Fénelon), prayer must of necessity pass through language.

The third operation is ordering: not merely to arrange the elementary signs, but to subject the vast erotic, eudaemonist, or mystical sequence to a higher order, no longer syntactical, but metrical; the new discourse is provided with an Ordainer, a Master of Ceremonies, a Rhetorician: in Ignatius, it is the retreat director, in Fourier some patron or matron, in Sade, some libertine who, with no standing other than a temporary and entirely practical responsibility, sets up the postures and directs the over-all progress of the erotic operation; there is always someone to regulate (but not: regiment) the exercise, séance, orgy, but that someone is not a subject; the producer of the episode, he acts only for the moment, he is merely a rective morpheme, an operator of the sequence. Thus the ritual demanded by our three authors is only a form of planning: it is the order necessary for pleasure, happiness, divine interlocution (just as any form of text is always only the ritual that orders pleasure); but this economy is not appropriative, it remains "excessive," it says only that unconditioned loss is not uncontrolled loss: loss must be ordered in order to become unconditional: the ultimate vacation, the denial of any reciprocal economy, is itself obtained only by means of an economy: Sadian ecstasy, Fourierist jubilation, Ignatian indifference, never exceed the language that constitutes them: isn't a materialist rite that one beyond which there is nothing?

Were logothesis to stop at setting up a ritual, i.e., a rhetoric, the founder of language would be no more than the author of a system (what is called a philosopher, a savant, or a thinker). Sade, Fourier, Loyola are something else: formulators (commonly called writers). In fact, to found a new language *through and through,* a fourth operation is required: *theatricalization.* What is theatricalization? It is not designing a setting for representation, but unlimiting the language. Although all three are committed, through historical position, to an ideology of representation and sign, what our logothetes produce is nonetheless already text; that is to say, that for platitude of style (as found in "great" writers), they have found a way to substitute volume of writing. The style supposes and practices the opposition of matter and form; it is the lamination of a substructure; the writing reaches a point at which it produces a row of signifiers, such that no language matter can still be recovered; because it is conceived as a "form," style implies a "consistency"; the writing, to use Lacan's term, only recognizes "instances." And this is what our three classifiers do: it makes little difference how their style is judged, good, bad, or indifferent: they persist, never stop the weighing and elaborating operation; as the style is absorbed in the writing, the system disintegrates into systematics, the novel into the novelistic, prayer into the fantasmatic: Sade is no longer an erotic, Fourier no longer a utopian, Loyola no longer a saint: all that is left in each of them is a scenographer: he who disperses himself across the framework he sets up and arranges *ad infinitum*.

Thus, if Sade, Fourier, and Loyola are founders of a language, and only that, it is precisely in order to say nothing, to observe a vacancy (if they wanted to say *something*, linguistic language, the language of communication and philosophy, would suffice: they could be *summarized,* which is not the case with any one of them). Language, the field of the signifier, presents instant, not consistent, relationships: center, weight, meaning are dismissed. The least-centered Logothesis is certainly that of Fourier (passions and stars are constantly being dispersed, apportioned), and this is undoubtedly why he is the most euphoric. For Loyola, of course, as we shall see, God is the Mark, the internal accent, the deep crease, and we will not dispute with the Church over this saint; however, caught up in the fury of the writing, this mark, this accent,

this crease are finally not enough: a formidably subtle, logo-
thetic system, through trickery, produces or tries to produce
semantic indifference, equality of interrogation, a mantic art
in which lack of response involves absence of the respondent.
And for Sade, there is something that balances the language
and makes it into a centered metonymy, but that something
is fucking ("All immoralities are connected and the closer we
come to the immorality of fucking the happier we will necessarily be"), i.e., literally, dissemination.

Nothing is more depressing than to imagine the Text as
an intellectual object (for reflection, analysis, comparison,
mirroring, etc.). The text is an object of pleasure. The bliss
of the text is often only stylistic: there are expressive felicities,
and neither Sade nor Fourier lacks them. However, at times
the pleasure of the Text is achieved more deeply (and then
is when we can truly say there is a Text): whenever the
"literary" Text (the Book) transmigrates into our life, whenever another writing (the Other's writing) succeeds in writing
fragments of our own daily lives, in short, whenever a *coexistence* occurs. The index of the pleasure of the Text, then,
is when we are able to live with Fourier, with Sade. To live
with an author does not necessarily mean to achieve in our
life the program that author has traced in his books (this conjunction is not, however, insignificant, since it forms the argument of *Don Quixote;* true, Don Quixote is still a character
in a book); it is not a matter of making operative what has
been represented, not a matter of becoming sadistic or orgiastic with Sade, a phalansterian with Fourier, of praying
with Loyola; it is a matter of bringing into our daily life the
fragments of the unintelligible ("formulae") that emanate
from a text we admire (admire precisely because it hangs
together well); it is a matter of speaking this text, not making
it act, by allowing it the distance of a citation, the eruptive
force of a coined word, of a language truth; our daily life

then itself becomes a theater whose scenery is our own social habitat; to live with Sade is, at times, to speak Sadian, to live with Fourier is to speak in Fourier (to live with Loyola?— why not?—once again, it is not a matter of taking into ourselves the contents, convictions, a faith, a cause, nor even images; it is a matter of receiving from the text a kind of fantasmatic order: of savoring with Loyola the sensual pleasure of organizing a retreat, of covering our interior time with it, of distributing in it moments of language: the bliss of the writing is barely mitigated by the seriousness of the Ignatian representations).

The pleasure of the Text also includes the amicable return of the author. Of course, the author who returns is not the one identified by our institutions (history and courses in literature, philosophy, church discourse); he is not even the biographical hero. The author who leaves his text and comes into our life has no unity; he is a mere plural of "charms," the site of a few tenuous details, yet the source of vivid novelistic glimmerings, a discontinuous chant of amiabilities, in which we nevertheless read death more certainly than in the epic of a fate; he is not a (civil, moral) person, he is a body. In the total disengagement from value produced by the pleasure of the Text, what I get from Sade's life is not the spectacle, albeit grandiose, of a man oppressed by an entire society because of his passion, it is not the solemn contemplation of a fate, it is, *inter alia,* that Provençal way in which Sade says "milli" (mademoiselle) Rousset, or milli Henriette, or milli Lépinai, it is his white muff when he accosts Rose Keller, his last games with the Charenton linen seller (in her case, I am enchanted by the linens); what I get from Fourier's life is his liking for *mirlitons* (little Parisian spice cakes), his belated sympathy for lesbians, his death among the flowerpots; what I get from Loyola's life are not the saint's pilgrimages, visions, mortifications, and constitutions, but only his "beautiful eyes, always a little filled with tears." For if, through a twisted dialectic, the Text, destroyer of all subject, contains a subject to love, that subject is dispersed, somewhat like the ashes we strew into the wind after death (the theme of the *urn* and the *stone,* strong closed objects, instructors of fate, will be contrasted with the *bursts* of memory, the erosion that leaves nothing but a few furrows of past life): were I a writer, and dead, how I would love it if my life, through the pains of some friendly and detached biographer, were to reduce itself to a few details, a few preferences, a few inflections, let us say: to "biographemes" whose distinction and mobility might go beyond any fate and come to touch, like Epicurean atoms, some future body, destined to the same dispersion; a marked life, in sum, as Proust succeeded in writing his in his work, or even a film, in the old style, in which there is no dialogue and the flow of images (that *flumen orationis* which perhaps is what makes up the "obscenities" of writing) is intercut, like the relief of hiccoughs, by the barely written darkness of the intertitles, the casual eruption of *another* signifier: Sade's white muff, Fourier's flowerpots, Ignatius's Spanish eyes.

"Only the bored have need of illusion," Brecht wrote. The pleasure of a reading guarantees its truth. Reading texts and not books, turning upon them a clairvoyance not aimed at discovering their secret, their "contents," their philosophy, but merely their happiness of writing, I can hope to release Sade, Fourier, and Loyola from their bonds (religion, utopia, sadism); I attempt to dissipate or elude the moral discourse that has been held on each of them; working, as they themselves worked, only on languages, I unglue the text from its purpose as a guarantee: socialism, faith, evil. Whence (at least such is the theoretical intent of these studies) I force the displacement (but not to suppress; perhaps even to accentuate) of the text's social responsibility. There are those who believe they can with assurance discuss the site of this responsibility: it would be the author, inserting that author into his period, his history, his class. But another site remains enigmatic, escapes for the time being any illumination: the site of the reading. This obscuration occurs at the very moment bourgeois ideology is being most vituperated, without ever wondering from which site it is being talked about or against: is it the site of a non-discourse ("Let's not talk, let's not write, let's militate")? is it that of a contra-discourse ("Let's discourse against class culture"), but then made up of what traits, what figures, what reasonings, what cultural residues? To act as though an innocent discourse could be held against ideology is tantamount to continuing to believe that language can be nothing but the neutral instrument of a triumphant content. In fact, today, there is no language site outside bourgeois ideology: our language comes from it, returns to it, remains closed up in it. The only possible rejoinder is neither confrontation nor destruction, but only theft: fragment the old text of culture, science, literature, and change its features according to formulae of disguise, as one disguises stolen goods. Faced with the old text, therefore, I try to efface the false sociological, historical, or subjective efflorescence of determinations, visions, projections; I listen to the message's transport, not the message, I see in the threefold work the victorious deployment of the significant text, the terrorist text, allowing the received meaning, the (liberal) repressive discourse that constantly attempts to recover it, slough itself off like an old skin. The social intervention of a text (not necessarily achieved at the time the text appears) is measured not by the popularity of its audience or by the fidelity of the socioeconomic reflection it contains or projects to a few eager sociologists, but rather by the violence that enables it to *exceed* the laws that a society, an ideology, a philosophy establish for themselves in order to agree among themselves in a fine surge of historical intelligibility. This excess is called: writing.

June 1971

Note

1. "Loyola" is only the name of a village. I know one should say "Ignatius" or "Ignatius Loyola," but I persist in speaking of this author as I have always named him for myself: the writer's orthonym is of small importance: he does not derive his name from the rules of onomastics, but from the community of labor in which he is caught.

2. "Sade I" appeared in *Tel Quel*, No. 28 (Winter 1967), under the title "L'Arbre du crime," and in Volume XVI of Sade's *Oeuvres complètes* (Paris: Cercle du Livre Précieux, 1967), pp. 509–32. "Loyola" appeared in *Tel Quel*, No. 38 (Summer 1969), entitled "Comment parler à Dieu?" and was intended as an introduction to *Exercices spirituels* translated by Jean Ristat, to be published by Christian Bourgois Publishers, Collection 10 × 18. "Fourier" appeared in part in *Critique*, No. 281 (October 1970), entitled "Vivre avec Fourier." Few changes have been made in these texts. "Sade II," a portion of "Fourier," and the "Life" of Sade are published here for the first time.

3. References are to: D. A. F. Sade, *Oeuvres complètes* (Paris: Cercle du Livre Précieux, 1967), 16 volumes. Charles Fourier, *Oeuvres complètes* (Paris: Edition Anthropos, 1967), 11 volumes. Ignatius Loyola, *Exercices spirituels*, translation by François Courel (Paris: Desclée de Brouwer, 1963), and *Journal spirituel*, translation by Maurice Giuliani (Desclée de Brouwer, 1959).

4. The facts set forth in the "Lives" are secondhand. For Sade, they come from Gilbert Lély's monumental biography of Sade (Paris: Cercle du Livre Précieux, 1966), Vols. I and II, and from Sade's *Journal inédit*, preface by Georges Daumas (Paris: Gallimard, Collection "Idées," paperback, 1970). For Fourier, the facts come from the prefaces of Simone Debout-Oleszkiewicz in Vols. I and VII of *Oeuvres complètes* of Fourier (Paris: Edition Anthropos, 1967).

5. I have not attempted a "Life" of Loyola. The reason for this is that I could never have written that "Life" in conformity with the *biographical* principles referred to in the preface; I lacked the significant material. This lack is a historical one, and I therefore have no reason to conceal it. There are in fact two hagiographies: that in

11

The Golden Legend (fifteenth century) amply allows the signifier to enter in and fill out the scene (the signifier, that is, the martyred body); that of Ignatius, modern, suppresses this same body: we know nothing of this saint but his misty eyes and his claudication. In the first book, the story of the life is based on the *given* of the body; in the second, it is its *not-given:* the gap between economy and sign, to be found in many other fields, in the storehouse of the Middle Ages and in modern times, also occurs in writing on sainthood. Beyond (or outside) the sign, toward the signifier, we know nothing of the life of Ignatius Loyola.

Ramon Alejandro has kindly made a drawing of the meeting hall of the Château de Silling, for which I am grateful.

SADE I

W E TRAVEL a great deal in some of Sade's novels. Juliette crosses (and devastates) France, Savoy, Italy as far as Naples; with Brisa-Testa, we reach Siberia, Constantinople. The voyage is a facile initiatory theme; nevertheless, although *Juliette* begins with an apprenticeship, the Sadian voyage teaches nothing (the diversity of customs being relegated to the Sadian dissertation, where it serves to prove that vice and virtue are completely local notions); whether Astrakhan, Angers, Naples, or Paris, cities are merely purveyors, countrysides are retreats, gardens are scenery, and climates are operators of lust;[1] it is always the same geography, the same population, the same functions; what must be gone through are not the more or less exotic contingencies, but the repetition of an essence, that of crime (and let us include in this word once and for all torture and debauchery). If, therefore, the voyage is varied, the Sadian site is unique: one travels only to shut oneself away. The model of the Sadian site is Silling, the château Durcet owns in the depths of the Black Forest, in which the four libertines of *The 120 Days* shut themselves away for four months with their harem. This château is hermetically isolated from the world by a series of obstacles that recall those found in certain fairy tales: a village of woodcutter-smugglers (who allow no one to pass), a steep mountain, a dizzy precipice which can be

[1] E.g., the Siberian snow, which serves for a special debauchery.

crossed only by a bridge (which the libertines destroy once they are inside), a thirty-foot wall, a deep moat, a door which is walled up as soon as they have entered, and lastly, a frightful lot of snow.

Thus the Sadian enclosure is relentless; it has a dual function; first, of course, to isolate, to shelter vice from the world's punitive attempts; yet libertine solitude is not merely a precaution of a practical nature; it is a quality of existence, a sensual pleasure of being;[2] e.g., it has a functionally useless but philosophically exemplary form: within the best-tested retreats, there always exists, in Sadian space, a "solitary" where the libertine takes some of his victims, far away from all, even friendly, eyes, where he is irrevocably alone with his object—a highly unusual thing in this communal society; this "solitary" is obviously formal, since what happens there, being on the order of torture or crime, very explicit practices in the Sadian world, has no reason to be hidden; excepting the religious "solitary" of Saint-Fond, the Sadian solitary is merely the theatrical form of solitude: for a time, it desocializes crime; in a world deeply penetrated by speech, it achieves a rare paradox: that of a silent act; and since in Sade there is never anything real save for the narration, the silence of "solitary" is completely confounded with the blank of the narrative: the meaning stops. This "hole" has as its analogous sign the very site of the solitaries: these are usually deep cellars, crypts, tunnels, excavations located deep within the châteaux, the gardens, the pits, from which one emerges alone, saying nothing.[3] Thus, the solitary place is a trip into the bowels of

[2] The snow falls on Silling: "One cannot imagine how sensual pleasure is served by such securities as one has when one can say, 'I am alone here, I am at the world's end, away from all eyes, and where no creature can get to me; no restraints, no barriers.'"

[3] The Gardens of the Société des Amis du Crime: "At the foot of certain of these trees pits have been dug into which the victim can suddenly disappear. Often one dines under these trees, sometimes in

the earth, a telluric theme to which Juliette gives meaning with regard to the Pietra Mala volcano.

The enclosure of the Sadian site has another function: it forms the basis of a social autarchy. Once shut in, the libertines, their assistants, and their subjects form a total society, endowed with an economy, a morality, a language, and a time articulated into schedules, labors, and celebrations. Here, as elsewhere, the enclosure permits the system, i.e., the imagination. The nearest equivalent to the Sadian city will be the Fourierist phalanstery: the same attempt to establish in every detail a human internship sufficient unto itself, the same determination to identify happiness with a completed and organized space, the same eagerness to define beings by their functions and to regulate the entry into play of those functioning classes according to a detailed scenario, the same attention to instituting an economy of the passions, in short, the same "harmony" and the same utopia. The Sadian utopia—like that of Fourier, for that matter—is measured far less against theoretical statements than against the organization of daily life, for the mark of utopia is the everyday; or even: everything everyday is utopian: timetables, dietary programs, plans for clothing, the installation of furnishings, precepts of conversation or communication, all that is in Sade: the Sadian city is based not solely on "pleasures," but also on needs: it is thus possible to sketch an ethnography of the Sadian village.

We know what the libertines eat. We know, for example, that on November 10, at Silling, the gentlemen refresh themselves at dawn with an improvised collation (the cooks having been awakened) consisting of scrambled eggs, chincara, onion soup, and omelettes. These details (and many more) ·

---

the pits themselves. Some of them are extremely deep and can be descended into only by secret stairways, and in which one can abandon oneself to every possible infamy with the same calm, the same silence, as if one were in the bowels of the earth."

are not set forth for nothing. In Sade, diet is a fact of caste, and therefore subject to classification. The libertine diet is both a sign of luxury, without which there can be no libertinism, not because luxury is pleasurable "in itself"—the Sadian system is not merely hedonistic—but because the money it takes ensures the division into poor and rich, slaves and masters: "I want always," says Saint-Fond, describing his table fare for Juliette, "the most exquisite dishes, the rarest wines, the most extraordinary game and fruits"; as well as, which is different, a sign of enormity, i.e., monstrosity: Minski, M. de Gernande (the libertine who bleeds his wife every four days), have fabulous meals whose fabulousness (dozens of courses, hundreds of dishes, a dozen bottles of wine, two of liqueurs, ten cups of coffee) attests to the powerful constitution of the libertine body. In addition, food, according to the master, has two functions. On the one hand, it is restorative, it replaces the vast quantities of sperm expended in the libertine's life; few are the parties that are not introduced by a meal and followed by a few "restorative comforts," chocolates or roasts with Spanish wine. Clairwil, whose debaucheries are gigantesque, follows a "wise" diet: she eats only boned game and fowl, in disguised form, her regular all-season drink is cold sugar water flavored with twenty drops of lemon essence and two spoonfuls of orange water. On the other hand, and inversely, when administered, food is used to poison or at least to neutralize: stramonium is introduced into Minski's chocolate to put him to sleep, poison into young Rose's and Mme de Bressac's to kill them. A substance either restorative or murderous, Sadian chocolate ends up by functioning as the pure sign of this dual alimentary economy.[4] Second-class food, that of the victims, is just as

---

[4] Restorative chocolate: "Everything is said: Monseigneur, worn out, goes back to bed, his chocolate is prepared for him," or: "After his orgy, the King of Sardinia offered me half his chocolate. I accepted, we talked politics. . . ."

ordinary: chicken and rice, compotes, chocolate (again!) for breakfast for Justine and her companions at the Benedictine monastery where they make up the harem. The victims' food is always copious, for two very libertine reasons: first, these victims too must be refreshed (Mme de Gernande, an angelic creature, having been bled, calls for partridges and *caneton de Rouen*) and fattened up to furnish vice with round, dimpled "altars"; second, coprophagic passion demands an "abundant, delicate, soft" food; whence a diet planned with medical precision (white meat, boned game, no bread, salt, or fat, feed often and quickly outside the regular mealtimes in order to bring on demi-indigestion, such as the recipe La Duclos gives). Thus, the functions of food in the Sadian city: to restore, to poison, to fatten, to evacuate; everything planned in relation to vice.

The same applies to clothing. This object, which can be said to be at the center of all of today's eroticism, from fashion to striptease, retains in Sade an unwaveringly functional value—which would already be enough to set its eroticism off from what we understand by this word. Sade does not play perversely (i.e., morally) with relationships between body and clothing. In the Sadian city, there are none of the allusions, provocations, and dodges we reserve for our clothing: love is immediately made naked; and as for the striptease, all we have is merely the brutal "Take it off!" with which the libertine commands his subject to assume a position in which to be examined.[5] Of course, the game of clothing exists in Sade; however, as with food, it is an explicit game of signs and functions. First signs: when in a group the naked brushes up against the clothed (and thereby contrasts with it), that is, outside of orgies, it serves to mark particularly

---

Killer chocolate: "When I have given Monsieur's dear son a good fucking, we will make him have a cup of chocolate in the morning. . . ."

[5] Save for one exception, to be mentioned later.

humiliated persons; during the great narrative scenes played out at Silling each evening, the entire harem is (provisionally) clothed, but the relatives of the four gentlemen, especially the debased wives and daughters, remain naked. As for clothing itself (and here we are talking only about that of the harems, the only one in which Sade is interested), it designates by means of planned artifices (colors, ribbons, garlands) either the classes of subjects: classes of age (how much this all, once again, makes us think of Fourier), classes of functions (boys and girls, fuckers, old women), classes of initiation (virgin subjects change their style of vestment after the ceremony of their defloration), classes of property (each libertine gives his stable a color);[6] or clothing is regulated according to its theatricality, it is endowed with those scenic protocols which, in Sade—outside the "solitary" we have mentioned—create the over-all ambiguity of the "scene," the ordered orgy and the cultural episode which derive from paintings of mythology, operatic finales, and set pieces of the Folies Bergère; its substance is thus usually brilliant and light (gauzes, taffetas), pink predominates, at least for the young subjects; thus the ethnic costumes worn at Silling each evening by the four (Asian, Spanish, Turkish, Greek) and the old women (gray nuns, fairies, sorceresses, widows). Beyond these signs, Sadian clothing is "functional," adapted to the services of vice: it must be instantly removable. One description joins all these characteristics: that of the clothing that the gentlemen of Silling give to their four favorite lovers: here we have a veritable building of costume, each detail of which is thought out in relation to its spectacle (a little tight vest, spicy and open like a Prussian uniform) and to its function (pants open in the back which will fall off in a second if the large knot of ribbons holding them on is pulled). The libertine

---

[6] Transvestism is rare in Sade. Juliette tries it once, but ordinarily it seems to be downgraded as a source of illusion (or is employed negatively, to determine subjects who will stand firm against it).

is a designer, or he is a dietician, architect, decorator, director, etc.

Since we are here engaged in a bit of human geography, a word should be said about the Sadian population. What are they like physically, these Sadianites? The libertine race only exists after thirty-five years of age;[7] totally repugnant if old (the most frequent case), libertines nevertheless sometimes have fine figures, fiery eyes, fresh breath, but this beauty is then counterbalanced by a cruel or wicked air. The subjects for debauchery are handsome if young, horrible if old, but in both cases useful for vice. Thus we see that in this "erotic" world neither age nor beauty enables us to determine classes of individuals. Classification is of course possible, but only at the level of the discourse: in fact, in Sade, there are two kinds of "portraits." The first are realistic, they painstakingly individualize their model, from face to sexual organs: "The President de Curval . . . was tall, dry, thin, his eyes sunken and dim, a pale and unsavory mouth, tilted chin, long nose. Covered with hair like a satyr, a flat back, flaccid pendulous buttocks which rather resembled a pair of dirty towels floating above his thighs," etc.: this portrait is "true" (in the sense this word can have as traditionally applied to literature) as to genre; it thus makes for diversity; on the one hand, every description becomes more detailed as one descends the length of the body, for it is in the author's interest to describe sexual organs and buttocks better than faces; and on the other hand, the libertine portrait must reveal the great morphological (but in no way functional, all libertines being both sodomites and sodomized) contrast between satyrs, dry and hairy (Curval, Blangis), and the cinedic cupids, white and plump (the Bishop, Durcet). Yet as one passes from the libertines to their assistants and then on to their victims, the portraits be-

---

[7] Juliette alone is very young; however, one must remember that she is an apprentice libertine—and that, furthermore, she is the subject of the narrative.

come unrealistic; thus we come to the second Sadian portrait: that of subjects for debauchery (and principally young girls); this portrait is purely rhetorical, a *topos*. Here is Alexandrine, Saint-Fond's daughter, decidedly too stupid for Juliette to complete her education: "The most sublime bosom, very pretty details in the forms, freshness of skin, disengagement of masses, grace, softness in the articulation of members, a celestial figure, the most flattering and interesting organ, and much romance in her spirit." These portraits are highly cultural, referring to painting ("fit for painting") or to mythology ("the form of Minerva with the charms of Venus"), which is a good way of making them abstract.[8] In fact, the rhetorical portrait, albeit oftentimes somewhat drawn out (for the author never loses interest), paints nothing, neither the thing nor its effect: it does not make visible (and certainly doesn't try); it characterizes very little (sometimes the color of the eyes, the hair); it is content with naming the anatomical elements, each of which is perfect; and since this perfection, in good theology, is the very essence of the thing, it suffices to say a body is perfect in order for it to be so: ugliness is describable, beauty is stated; these rhetorical portraits are therefore empty exactly insofar as they are portraits of being; the libertines, although they can be subjected to a certain typology, are in the event, since they thus give rise to ever new portraits; however, since the victims are in being, they can encounter only empty signs, can inspire always only the same portrait, which affirms them, but does not embody them. Thus it is neither ugliness nor beauty, it is the very instance of the discourse, divided into

---

[8] Moral detail, mingled with physical detail, is functional: just as wit, intelligence, imagination make good libertines, so do sensibility, vivacity, romance, religion make good victims. For that matter, Sade recognizes only one form of energy, whether physical or moral: "We shall feed her ecstasy . . . by caressing her with all our physical and moral means," Juliette says apropos La Durand. And: "I was naked, I no longer existed save through the profound awareness of my vice."

figure portraits and sign portraits, that determines the grouping of Sadian humanity.[9]

This grouping does not include social division, although Sade is not oblivious to it. Victims are of every rank, and if noble subjects are given a kind of primacy of rank, it is because "bon ton" is a prime operator of vice,[10] owing to the victim's increased humiliation: in Sadian practice, there is a positive amusement to be gained from sodomizing the daughter of a Parliamentary counselor, or a young Knight of Malta. And if the masters themselves always belong to the upper classes (princes, popes, bishops, nobles, or wealthy commoners), it is because one cannot be a libertine without money. However, Sadian money has two different functions. First, it appears to play a practical role, it allows for the purchase and upkeep of the harems: pure means, it is then neither prized nor disprized; one only hopes it will not form an obstacle to libertinage; thus, in the Société de Amis du Crime, there is provision for a reduction in price for a contingent of twenty artists or men of letters who are known to be of modest means, to whom "society, protectress of the arts, wishes to offer this deference" (today, we could get in for four million légers a year). However, as we might expect, money is far more than a means: it is an honor, it clearly designates the evildoers and criminals who are permitted to accumulate it (Saint-Fond, Minski, Noirceuil, the four protagonists in *The 120 Days,* Juliette herself). Money proves vice and supports bliss: not because it procures pleasures (for Sade, what "gives pleasure" is never there "for pleasure"), but because it guarantees the spectacle of poverty; Sadian society is not cynical, it is cruel; it does not say: there must be poor in

[9] The same contrast with regard to proper names. The libertines and their assistants have "realistic" names, whose "truth" would not be disallowed by Balzac, Zola, etc. The victims have stage names.

[10] Girls having "bon ton" form a specific class of vice, as do young men, ugly girls, and virgins.

order that there be rich; it says the opposite: there must be rich in order that there be poor; wealth is necessary because it contrasts with misfortune. When Juliette, following Clairwil's example, shuts herself away from time to time to count her gold, with a jubilation that drives her to ecstasy, she is not contemplating the sum of her possible pleasures, but the sum of her accomplished crimes, the common poverty, positively refracted in this gold which, being there, cannot be elsewhere; money, therefore, in no way designates what it can acquire (not a *value*), but what it can withhold (a site of separation).

To have, in sum, is essentially to be able to consider those who have not. This formal grouping of course includes the libertines and their objects. As we know, there are two great classes of Sadian society. These classes are set, one cannot emigrate from one to another; no social promotion. And yet, it is essentially an educative society, or more exactly a school society (and even a boarding-school society); however, Sadian education does not play the same role with regard to victims and their masters. The former are often subjected to courses in libertinage, but they are, shall one say, technical courses (lessons in masturbation every morning at Silling), not philosophical; school endows the small victim society with its system of punishments, injustices, and hypocritical harangues (the prototype of which, in *Justine,* is the establishment of Rodin the surgeon, at once school, harem, and vivisection laboratory). For the libertines, the educative project has another dimension: they arrive at the absolute of libertinage: Clairwil is assigned to Juliette, although the latter is already quite far advanced, as her professor, and Juliette herself is given by Saint-Fond the task of acting as preceptress to his daughter Alexandrine. The mastery sought here is not that of philosophy: the education is not of this or that character, but of the reader. In any event, education never permits crossing over from one class to another: Justine, lectured to so often, never leaves her victim status.

In this highly coded society, communications (the most rigid society cannot do without them) are assured not by movement, but by a system of relays which are also rigid. Here, in its furthest extension, is how we can set up the scale of Sadian society: (1) the great libertines (Clairwil, Olympe Borghèse, La Delbène, Saint-Fond, Noirceuil, the four leaders of *The 120 Days,* the King of Sardinia, Pope Pius VI and his cardinals, the King and Queen of Naples, Minski, Brisa-Testa, the counterfeiter Roland, Cordelli, La Gernande, Bressac, various monks, priests, Parliamentary counselors, etc.); (2) the major assistants, who form the bureaucracy of libertinage, include the female narrators and the great procuresses like La Duvergier; (3) next the aides; sorts of housekeepers or duennas, half domestics half subjects (La Lacroix, who assists the aged Archbishop of Lyons, simultaneously serves him his chocolate and her rear end), or confidential menservants, torturers, or pimps; (4) the subjects *per se* are either occasional (families, young children fallen into the hands of the libertines) or regular, brought together in harems; distinction should be made between the principal patients, who are the objects of particular séances, and the *jokers,* something like overseers of the debauchery, who accompany the libertine everywhere to comfort or distract him; (5) the last class, or pariah class, is made up of wives. From one class to another, the individuals have no relationship (save that of libertine practices); however, the libertines themselves communicate in two ways: through contracts (the one linking Juliette to Saint-Fond is very detailed) or pacts: the pact between Juliette and Clairwil is marked by deep, ardent friendship. Contracts and pacts are at once eternal ("This is an adventure that joins us for life") and revocable from one day to the next: Juliette shoves Olympe Borghèse into Vesuvius and ends by poisoning Clairwil.

Thus, the principal protocols of Sadian society; each, we have seen, attests to the same grouping, that of libertines and

victims. Yet, although to be expected, this grouping is yet
not founded: all the traits that separate the two classes are
effects of the grouping, but do not determine it. What then
makes the master? What makes the victim? Is it the practice
of vice (since it forces the separation of agents and patients), as has been commonly held ever since Sadian society's laws created what is called "sadism"? We must now
investigate the *praxis* of this society, it being understood that
every *praxis* is itself a code of meaning,[11] and that it can be
analyzed by units and by regulations.

Sade, we have been constantly told, is an "erotic" author.
But what is eroticism? It is never more than a word, since
practices cannot be so coded unless they are known, i.e.,
spoken;[12] now, our society never utters any erotic practice,
only desires, preliminaries, contexts, suggestions, ambiguous
sublimations, so that, for us, eroticism cannot be defined save
by a perpetually elusive word. On this basis, Sade is not
erotic: it has been remarked that in his case there is never
any kind of striptease, that apologue essential to modern
eroticism.[13] It is completely improperly, and with immense
presumption, that our society speaks of Sade's eroticism, that
is, of a system for which it has no equivalent. The difference

[11] For Aristotle, *praxis,* practical science which produces no work
distinct from the agent (in contrast to *poiesis*), is based on the
rational choice between two possible modes of action, or *proairesis:*
this, obviously, is already a coded concept of *praxis.* We will re-en-
counter this concept of praxis as a language in the modern concept of
strategy.

[12] It goes without saying that erotic language is elaborated not only
in articulated language but also in the language of images.

[13] Here is the exception mentioned, the only adumbration of Sadian
striptease (young Rose, brought to Saint-Fond's): "Take her panties
off for me, Juliette, lift her skirt above her waist, letting her panties
drop down her thighs agreeably; I am mad about an ass offered
in this way."

arises not because Sadian eroticism is criminal and ours harmless, but because the former is assertive, combinatory, whereas ours is suggestive, metaphorical. For Sade, there is no eroticism unless the crime is "reasoned";[14] *to reason* means to philosophize, to dissertate, to harangue, in short, to subject crime (a generic term designating all the Sadian passions) to a system of articulated language; but it also means to combine according to precise rules the specific actions of vice, so as to make from these series and groups of actions a new "language," no longer spoken but acted; a "language" of crime, or new code of love, as elaborate as the code of courtly love.

Sadian practice is ruled by a great notion of order: "irregularities" are strenuously regulated, vice is unbridled but not without order (at Silling, for example, all debauchery irrevocably ends at 2 A.M.). Expressions describing a purposeful structuring of the erotic scene are innumerable and constant: *dispose the group, arrange everything, execute a new scene, make a libidinous act out of three scenes, form the newest and most libertine tableau, make a little scene out of that, everything falls into place;* or, on the other hand: *disarrange all the poses, break up the poses, everything will change soon, change the pose,* etc. Ordinarily, Sadian combinativity is determined by an ordinator (a director): " 'Friends,' the monk said, 'let us put some order into these proceedings,' " or: "Here is how the whore disposed the group." In no case may the erotic order be bypassed: " 'One moment,' La Delbène said, all flushed, 'one second, my fine friends, let's put a little order into our pleasures, we can only enjoy them by fixing them' "; whence a highly comical ambiguity between the libertine admonition and the professorial apostrophe, the harem being always a miniature classroom (" 'One moment,

[14] In the Siberian desert, Brisa-Testa encounters only one libertine, the Hungarian Tergowitz: "That one at least reasoned crime."

one moment, young ladies,' La Delbène said, trying to re-establish order . . ."). However, sometimes the erotic order is institutional: only custom controls it: the libertine nuns in a Bolognese convent practice a collective figure called the "rosary" in which the ordinators are old nuns placed after each decade (which is why each of these directrices is called an *Our Father*). Or sometimes, more mysteriously, the erotic order is self-established, be it pre-existing injunction, be it collective prescience of what must be done, be it knowledge of the structural laws that prescribe the completion of an initi-ated figure in a certain way; this subjected and apparently spontaneous order, Sade indicates with a phrase: *the scene goes on, the tableau falls into place.* So that in the presence of the Sadian scene a powerful impression is created, not of au-tomatism, but of "scrupulosity," or, if one prefers, of per-formance.

The erotic code consists of units which have been carefully determined and named by Sade himself. The minimal unit is the *posture;* it is the smallest combination that can be imagined, for it unites only one action and its bodily point of application; since neither these actions nor these points are infinite, far from it, the postures can easily be enumerated, which we shall not do here; it will suffice to indicate that aside from strictly sexual acts (permitted and prohibited), we must include in this first inventory all actions and every site capable of arousing the libertine's "imagination," not always recorded by Krafft-Ebing, such as the examination of the victim, his interrogation, blasphemy, etc.; and that on the level of simple elements of posture one must place the particular "operators" such as family ties (incest or conjugal vexation), social rank (of which we have spoken), hideousness, filth, psychological states, etc. Since posture is a basic formation, it is inevitably repeated and thus it can be submitted to accountancy; after an orgy including Juliette, Clairwil, and the Carmelites one Easter, Juliette does her accounts: she has been had 128 times one way, 128 times another way, thus 256 times in all, etc.[15] Combined, postures compose a unit of higher rank, the *operation*. The operation calls, at least most frequently, for several actors; when it is conceived as a tableau, a simultaneous ensemble of postures, it is called a *figure;* when on the contrary it is conceived as a diachronic unit, developing in time through a succession of postures, it is called an *episode*. What limits (and constitutes) the episode are the constraints of time (the episode is contained between two ejaculations); what limits the figure are the constraints of space (all erotic sites must be simultaneously occupied). Finally, operations, extending and succeeding each other, form the largest possible unit of this erotic grammar, the "scene" or "séance." The scene over, we return to narrative or to dissertation.

All these units are subject to rules of combination—or composition. These rules may readily permit a formalization of the erotic language, analogous to the diagrammatic "trees" proposed by our linguists: in sum, this would be the tree of crime.[16] Sade himself did not disdain algorism, as we see in Story 46 in the second part of *The 120 Days*.[17] In Sadian grammar there are two principal rules of action: they are, we might say, the regular procedures by which the narrator mobilizes the units of his "lexicon" (postures, figures, episodes). The first is a rule of exhaustiveness: in an "operation," the greatest number of postures must be simultaneously achieved; this implies on the one hand that every actor present be occupied at the same time, and if possible in the same group (or in any case in groups which recur);[18] and on the

[15] Juliette's imagination is eminently that of a bookkeeper: at one point she plans a numerical project designed for the certain corruption, by geometrical progression, of the entire French population.

[16] ". . . The branches of crime in this whole adventure are pretty enough . . ." (*Juliette*).

[17] "He makes girl A shit, then B; then he forces B . . ." etc.

[18] The paroxysmal example would be the scene in which Bracciani

other hand, that in each subject every part of the body be erotically saturated; the group is a kind of chemical nucleus, each "valence" of which must remain free: all of Sadian syntax is thus in search of the total figure. This relates to the panic character of libertinage; it does not recognize either idleness or repose; when libertine energy cannot be devoted to either scenes or harangues, it nonetheless observes a kind of shipboard schedule: this is the "teasing," a continual series of minor vexations to which the libertine subjects the objects that surround him. The second rule of action is the rule of reciprocity. First, of course, a figure can invert itself: such a combination, invented by Belmor, who applies it to girls, is varied by Noirceuil, who applies it to boys ("Let's give this fantasy another twist"). And above all, in Sadian grammar there are no reservations regarding any function whatsoever (with the exception of torture). In the scene, all functions can be interchanged, everyone can and must be in turn agent and patient, whipper and whipped, coprophagist and coprophagee, etc. This is a cardinal rule, first because it assimilates Sadian eroticism into a truly formal language, where there are only classes of actions, not groups of individuals, which enormously simplifies its grammar: the subject of the action (in the grammatical sense) can just as readily be a libertine, an assistant, a victim, a wife; second, because it keeps us from basing the grouping of Sadian society on the particularity of sexual practices (just the opposite of what occurs in our own society; we always wonder whether a homosexual is "active" or "passive"; with Sade, sexual preference never serves to identify a subject). Since everyone can be either sodomist or sodomized, agent and patient, subject and object, since pleasure is possible anywhere, with victims as well as masters,

---

and Chigi (cardinals of Pius VI), Olympe Borghèse, Juliette, the confederates, a monkey, a turkey, a dwarf, a child, and a dog form a group difficult to amplify.

we must look elsewhere for the rationale behind the Sadian grouping, which the ethnography of this society has not thus far enabled us to discover.

In fact, and this is the time to say it, aside from murder there is but one trait the libertines themselves possess and never share, in any form whatever: speech. The master is he who speaks, who disposes of the entirety of language; the object is he who is silent, who remains separate, by a mutilation more absolute than any erotic torture, from any access to discourse, because he does not even have any right to receive the master's word (the harangues are addressed solely to Juliette and to Justine, who is an ambiguous victim, endowed with narrative speech). Of course there are some victims— very few—who can gripe about their condition, represent the libertine's infamy to him (M. de Cloris, Mlle Fontange, de Donis, Justine); but they are only mechanical voices, they merely act as accomplices in filling out libertine speech. And only this speech is free, invented, completely blended into the energy of vice. In the Sadian city, speech is perhaps the sole caste privilege that cannot be curtailed. The libertine enjoys its entire gamut, from the silence in which the telluric eroticism of "solitary" is practiced, to the convulsions of speech that accompany ecstasy—and all its uses (orders for operations, blasphemies, harangues, dissertations); he can even, supreme ownership, delegate it (to the storytellers). Speech is wholly bound together with the overt mark of the libertine, which is (in Sade's vocabulary) the *imagination:* it might almost be said that *imagination* is the Sadian word for *language*. Fundamentally, the agent is not he who has power or pleasure, but he who controls the direction of the scene and the sentence (we know that every Sadian scene is the sentence of an other language) or: the direction of meaning. Beyond the characters of the anecdote, beyond Sade himself, the "subject" of Sadian eroticism thus is not, cannot be, anyone other than the "subject" of the Sadian sentence: the two instances, of the scene and of the discourse, have the same basis, the same rection, since the scene is merely discourse. We better understand now upon what and toward what Sade's erotic combinative rests and tends: its origin and its sanctions are rhetorical.

Indeed, the two codes, that of the sentence (oratorical) and that of the figure (erotic), continually relay each other, form one same line, along which the libertine travels with the same energy: the second indiscriminately prepares for or prolongs the first,[19] sometimes even accompanies it.[20] In short, speech and posture are of exactly the same value, one equals the other: giving one, we can get the other back in change: Belmor, appointed president of the Société des Amis du Crime, and having delivered a fine speech, a sixty-year-old man stops him and, to show his enthusiasm and gratitude, "begs him to give him his ass" (which Belmor hardly refuses to do). Thus it is not at all surprising that, anticipating Freud, but also inverting him, Sade makes sperm the substitute for speech (and not the opposite), describing it in the same terms applied to the orator's art: "Saint-Fond's discharge was brilliant, audacious, passionate," etc. Above all, however, the meaning of the scene is possible because the erotic code benefits totally from the logic of the language, manifested through the artifices of syntax and rhetoric. The sentence (its ellipses, its internal correlations, its figures, its sovereign progress) is what looses the surprises of the erotic combinative and converts the network of crime into a marvelous tree: "He says

[19] La Delbène and Juliette: "And her caresses becoming more ardent, we soon lit the flame of passion from the torch of philosophy." And elsewhere: "You have killed me with voluptuousness. Let's sit down and discuss."

[20] "I want to fondle your cocks while I talk . . . I want the energy they draw from my fingers to communicate itself to my discourse, and you will see my eloquence grow, not like Cicero's because of the movement of the crowds around the speaker's tribune, but like Sappho's, according to the fucking she was getting from Demophiles."

he knew a man who had fucked three children he had had with his mother, whence he had a daughter he had married to his son, so that by fucking her he was fucking his sister, his daughter, and his daughter-in-law, and he was making his son fuck his sister and his stepmother." The combinative (here parental) presents itself, in sum, as a complicated detour along which one feels oneself lost, but which all of a sudden comes together and lights up: starting with various actors, that is, from an unintelligible reality, we emerge through a trick of the sentence, *and precisely owing to that sentence*, onto a condensation of incest, i.e., onto a meaning. We can say finally that Sadian crime exists only in proportion to the quantity of language invested in it, in no way because it is dreamt or narrated, but because only language can construct it. Sade states at one point: "To bring together incest, adultery, sodomy, and sacrilege, he buggers his married daughter with a host." The nomenclature is what permits the parental foreshortening: the tree of crime springs out of the simple constatory utterance.

In short, therefore, all of Sade is supported on the writing of Sade. Its task, at which it is brilliantly successful, is to contaminate reciprocally the erotic and the rhetoric, speech and crime, to introduce suddenly into the conventions of social language the subversions of the erotic scene, at the same time as the "price" of this scene is deducted from the treasury of the language. This can clearly be seen at the level of what is traditionally called style. We know that in *Justine* the code of love is metaphorical: there is talk of the myrtles of Cytherea and the roses of Sodom. In *Juliette,* on the other hand, the erotic nomenclature is a naked one. The crux of the following passage is clearly not the crudity, the obscenity of the language, but the perfection of another rhetoric. Sade commonly practices what we might term metonymic violence: in the same syntagm he juxtaposes heterogeneous fragments belonging to spheres of language that are ordinarily kept separate by socio-moral taboo. Thus the Church, "fine" style, and pornography: "Yes, yes, Monseigneur," La Lacroix says to the aged Archbishop of Lyons, he of the fortifying choco- late, "and Your Eminence can plainly see that by exposing to him only the part he desires I am offering for his libertine homage the prettiest virgin ass hole to be kissed that there is."[21] What are here being overturned are obviously, in a very classical way, the social fetishes, kings, ministers, ecclesiastics, etc., but so too the language, the traditional classes of writ- ing: criminal contamination touches every style of the dis- course: narrative, lyrical, moral, maxim, mythological *topos*. We begin to recognize that the transgressions of language possess an offensive power at least as strong as that of moral transgressions, and that the "poetry" which is itself the language of the transgressions of language, is thereby always contestatory. In this light, not only is Sade's writing poetic, but in addition he has taken every precaution to see that this poetry is uncompromising: today's pornography can never recapture a world that exists in proportion to its writing, and society can never condone a writing structurally linked to crime and to sex.

Thus the singularity of the Sadian work is established— and at the same time, the forbidden which marks it is adum- brated: the city established by Sade, which we thought at the outset we would be able to describe as an "imaginary" city, with its time, its customs, its population, its habits, that city is entirely supported on words, not because it is the creation

[21] Innumerable examples of this process: "Papal passion, ministerial spanking, prime manipulation of the pontifical ass, sodomize his teacher," etc. (a process continued by Klossovski: the Inspectress's panties). The rules of agreement of tense can come into play, even if the effect is merely comic for us: "I should have liked to have had you kiss my Lubin's ass." It must be remembered that if we appear to hold Sade responsible for effects which historically he could not fore- see, it is because for us Sade is not the name of a person, but of an "author," or better yet, of a mythic "narrator," the depository over the years of all the meanings that his discourse has taken on.

of a novelist (a banal situation), but because inside the Sadian novel itself there is another book, a textual book, textured of pure writing, which determines everything that happens "imaginarily" in the first: not to tell, but to tell that one is telling. This fundamental situation of writing has as its very clear apologue the very argument of *The 120 Days of Sodom:* we know that at the Château of Silling the entire Sadian city—condensed into this site—is turned toward the *story* (or group of stories) solemnly delivered each night by the priestesses of speech, the storytellers.[22] This narrative pre-eminence is established by very precise protocols: the whole of the day's schedule converges toward its prime moment (evening), which is the story séance; it is prepared for, everyone must attend (excepting the agents on night duty); the assembly hall is a semicircular theater in the center of which is the storyteller's raised chair; below this throne of speech, the subjects of debauchery are seated, at the disposition of any gentleman who may wish to try out with them the proposals advanced by the storyteller; their status is fairly ambiguous, in the Sadian fashion, since they simultaneously constitute the units of the erotic figure and those of the speech being uttered over their heads: an ambiguity which affects everyone in his status as *example* (of grammar and of debauchery): practice follows speech, and is absolutely determined by it: what is done has been said.[23] Without formative speech, debauchery, crime, would be unable to invent themselves, to develop: the book must precede the book, the storyteller is the only "actor" in the book, since speech is its sole drama. The foremost of the storytellers, La Duclos, is the only creature in the libertine world to whom respect is shown: what one respects in her is *at once* crime and speech.

Now, in what only seems a paradox, it is perhaps on the

22 Juliette is also called a storyteller.
23 The crime has exactly the same dimension as the word: when the storytellers reach the murderous passions, the harem will be depopulated.

basis of the strictly *literary* make-up of the Sadian work that a particular quality of the interdictions upon it can be best observed. It often happens that the moral reprobation aimed against Sade is expressed in the form of aesthetic disgust: we declare that Sade is *monotonous*. Although every creation is of necessity combinative, society, by virtue of the old romantic myth of "inspiration," cannot stand being told so. Yet this is what Sade has done: he has opened and revealed his work (his "world") like the interior of a language, thereby accomplishing that union of a work and its criticism which Mallarmé so clearly rendered for us. But this is not all: the Sadian combinative (which is in no way, as has been said, that of *all* erotic literature) can seem monotonous to us only if we arbitrarily shift our reading from the Sadian discourse to the "reality" it is supposed to represent or imagine: Sade is boring only if we fix our gaze on the crimes being reported and not on the performances of the discourse.

Likewise, when, no longer invoking the monotony of Sadian criticism, but more frankly the "monstrous turpitudes" of an "abominable author," we come, as does the law, to ban Sade for moral reasons, it is because we refuse to enter the sole Sadian universe, which is the universe of the discourse. Yet on every page of his work, Sade provides us with evidence of concerted "irrealism": what happens in a novel by Sade is strictly fabulous, i.e., impossible; or more exactly, the impossibilities of the referent are turned into possibilities of the discourse, constraints are shifted: the referent is totally at the discretion of Sade, who can, like any narrator, give it fabulous dimensions, but the sign, belonging to the order of the discourse, is intractable, it makes the laws. For example: in a single scene, Sade multiplies the libertine's ecstasies beyond anything possible: one must, if one is to describe many figures in one lone séance: better to multiply ecstasies, referential units which consequently cost nothing, than scenes, which are units of discourse and consequently cost a great deal. Being a writer and not a realistic author, Sade always chooses the discourse over the referent; he always sides with *semiosis* rather than *mimesis:* what he "represents" is constantly being deformed by the meaning, and it is on the level of the meaning, not of the referent, that we should read him.

Which the society that bans him evidently does not do; it sees in Sade's work only the summoning forth of the referent; for it, the word is nothing but a window looking out onto the real; the creative process it envisions and upon which it bases its laws has only two terms: the "real" and its expression. The legal condemnation brought against Sade is therefore based on a certain system of literature, and this system is that of realism: it postulates that literature "represents," "figures," "imitates"; that the conformity of this imitation is what is being offered for judgment, aesthetic if the object is emotive, instructive or penal if it is monstrous; lastly, that to imitate is to persuade, to seduce: a schoolroom viewpoint with which, however, an entire society, and its institutions, agrees. Juliette, "proud and fresh in the world, soft and submissive in pleasure," is enormously seductive; however, the one who seduces me is the paper Juliette, the storyteller who makes herself a subject of the discourse, not a subject of "reality." Faced with La Durand's excesses, Juliette and Clairwil say these profound words: "Are you afraid of me?—Afraid, no; but we do not conceive you." Not conceivable *in* reality, *were she imaginary,* La Durand (like Juliette) becomes so as soon as she leaves the anecdotal instance to attain the instance of the discourse. The function of the discourse is not in fact to create "fear, shame, envy, an impression," etc., but to conceive the inconceivable, i.e., to leave nothing outside the words and to concede nothing ineffable to the world: such it seems is the keynote repeated throughout the Sadian city, from the Bastille where Sade existed only by words, to the Château of Silling, the sanctuary not of debauchery, but of the "story."

LOYOLA

The Writing

THE JESUITS, as we know, have contributed much to forming our notion of literature. The heirs and propagators of Latin rhetoric, through teaching, over which they had in the past, to all intents and purposes, a monopoly in Europe, they left bourgeois France with the concept of "fine writing," censure of which is still frequently confounded with the image of literary creation we set up. However, the Jesuits stubbornly deny to their founder's book this literary prestige they have helped to establish: the exposition of the *Exercises* is said to be "disconcerting," "curious," "bizarre"; "it is all labored," one Father writes, "literarily impoverished. The author has tried merely to provide the most just expression, the most exact transmission possible to the Society of Jesus, and thereby, to the Church, of the gift which he himself had received from God." Here we find once more the old modern myth according to which language is merely the docile and *insignificant* instrument for the serious things that occur in the spirit, the heart or the soul. This myth is not innocent; discrediting the form serves to exalt the importance of the content: to say: *I write badly* means: *I think well.* Classical ideology practices in the cultural order the same economy as bourgeois democracy does in the political order: a separation and a balance of powers, a broad but closely watched territory is conceded to literature, on condition that the territory be isolated, hierarchically, from other domains; thus it is that literature, whose function is a worldly one, is not

39

compatible with spirituality; one is detour, ornament, veil, the other is immediation, nudity: this is why one cannot be both a saint and a writer. Purified of any contact with the seductions and illusions of form, Ignatius's text, it is suggested, is barely language: it is the simple, neuter path which assures the transmission of a mental experience. Thus once again the place our society assigns to language is confirmed: decoration or instrument, it is seen as a sort of parasite of the human subject, who uses it or dons it at a distance, like an ornament or tool picked up and laid down according to the needs of subjectivity or the conformities of sociality.

However, another notion of writing is possible: neither decorative nor instrumental, i.e., in sum secondary but primal, antecedent to man, whom it traverses, founder of its acts like so many inscriptions. It is thus ridiculous to measure writing by its attributes (declaring it to be "rich," "sober," "poor," "curious," etc.). The only thing that counts is the assertion of its being, that is, in sum, its seriousness. Indifferent to suitabilities of genres, subjects, and ends, the seriousness of the form, which is not the "spirit of the serious," has nothing to do with the arrangement of "fine" works; it can even be wholly parodistic and make fun of the divisions and hierarchies our society, for conservationist ends, imposes on language acts. "Spiritual" as it may be, Ignatius's *Exercises* is based in writing. One need not be a Jesuit, a Catholic, a Christian, a believer, or a humanist to be interested in it. If we want to read Ignatius's discourse with this reading, interior to writing and not to faith, perhaps there is even some advantage in not being any of the above: the few lines Georges Bataille has written on the *Exercises*[1] have their weight, too, against the 1,500 or so commentaries inspired, since its first appearance, by this "universally extolled" manual of asceticism.

[1] In *L'Expérience intérieure* (Paris: Gallimard, 1954), p. 26.

The Multiple Text

Our reading habits, our very concept of literature, make every text appear today as if it were the simple communication of an author (in the present instance this Spanish saint who founded the Society of Jesus in the sixteenth century) and of a reader (in the present instance, ourselves): Ignatius Loyola wrote a book, this book was published, and today we are reading it. This outline, suspect for any book (since we can never definitively demonstrate *who* is the author and *who* is the reader), is assuredly false with regard to the *Exercises.* For if it is true that a text is defined through the unity of its communication, we are not reading *one* text, but rather *four* texts, disposed in the shape of the small book in our hands.

The first text is the one Ignatius addresses to the director of the retreat. This text represents the literal level of the work, its objective, historical nature: in fact, criticism assures us that the *Exercises* was not written for the retreatants themselves, but for their directors. The second text is the one the director addresses to the exercitant; the relationship of the two interlocutors is different here; it is no longer a relationship of reading or even of instruction, but of donation, implying credit on the part of the receiver, help and neutrality on the part of the donor, as in the case of psychoanalyst and analysand: the director *gives* the *Exercises* (virtually, as one *gives* food—or a whipping), he manages the material and adapts it so that he may transmit it to single organisms (at least this is how it used to be: today it seems the *Exercises* are given in a group). A maniable material, which can be elongated, shortened, softened, hardened, this second text is in a way the contents of the first (thus it can be called the semantic text); by that, we mean that if the first text constitutes the proper level of the discourse (as we read it), the second text is like the argument; and it follows that there need not necessarily be the same order: thus, in the first text the

Annotations precede the four Weeks: this is the order of the discourse; in the second text these same Annotations, bearing on the matters that can continuously concern the four Weeks, are not anterior to them, but somehow parametric, which attests to the independence of the two texts. This is not all. The first and second texts had a common actor: the director of the retreat, here receiver, there donor. Similarly, the exercitant is going to be both receiver and sender; having received the second text, he writes with it a third, which is an *acted* text made up of the meditation, gestures, and practices given him by his director: it is in a way the exercising of the *Exercises,* different from the second text insofar as he can detach himself from it by imperfectly accomplishing it. To whom is this third text addressed, this speech elaborated by the exercitant on the basis of the preceding texts? It can be no other than the Divinity. God is the receiver of a language whose speech here is prayers, colloquia, and meditations; furthermore, each exercise is explicitly preceded by a prayer addressed to God asking Him to receive the message that will follow: essentially an allegorical message, since it consists of images and imitations. To this language, the Divinity is called upon to respond: there thus exists, woven into the letter of the *Exercises,* a reply from God, of which God is the donor and the exercitant the receiver: fourth text, strictly anagogic, since we must trace back from stage to stage, from the letter of the *Exercises* to its contents and then to their action, before attaining the deepest meaning, the sign liberated by the Divinity.

As can be seen, the multiple text of the *Exercises* is a structure, i.e., an intelligent form: a structure of meanings, first, since we can find in it this diversity and this "perspective" of languages which has marked the relationship established between God and His creation through the theological thinking of the Middle Ages and which can be seen in the theory of the four meanings of the Scriptures; then a structure of inter-

I Literal Text	II Semantic	III Allegorical	IV Anagogic
Ignatius			
The Director	The Director		
	The Exercitant	The Exercitant	
		The Divinity	The Divinity
			The Exercitant

locution (and this is obviously more important), since of the four interlocutors set forth in the text, each save Ignatius assumes a dual role, being here sender and there receiver (yet Ignatius, who initiates the chain of messages, is basically nothing but the exercitant who ends it: he often administered the *Exercises* to himself, and to know the language the Divinity employs in its reply, one must refer to the *Spiritual Journal,* of which Ignatius is particularly the subject). Thus we are dealing with a structure made up of relays in which each one receives and transmits. What is the function of this dilatory structure? It is to establish at each relay of the interlocution two incertitudes. The first arises because, the *Exercises* being addressed to the director and not to the retreatant, the latter cannot (and must not) know in advance anything about the series of experiments which are gradually being recommended to him; he is in the situation of a reader of a narrative who is kept in suspense, a suspense which vitally concerns him, since he is also an actor in the story whose elements are gradually being given him. As for the second incertitude, it intervenes at the second relay of the fourfold text; it consists of the fol-

lowing: will the Divinity accept the language of the exercitant
and offer him in return a language to be deciphered? It is because of these two incertitudes, which are properly structural,
since they are established and intended by the structure, that
the multiple text of the *Exercises* is dramatic. Here the drama
is that of interlocution; on the one hand, the exercitant is like
a subject speaking in ignorance of the end of the sentence
upon which he has embarked; he lives the inadequacy of the
spoken chain, the opening of the syntagm, he is cut off from
the perfection of language, which is assertive closure; and
on the other hand, the very basis of all speech, interlocution
is not given him, he must conquer it, invent the language in
which he must address the Divinity and prepare his possible
response: the exercitant must accept the enormous and yet
uncertain task of a constructor of language, of a logo-techni-
cian.

Mantic Art

The notion of subjecting religious meditation to a method-
ology was not new; Ignatius could have inherited it from the
devotio moderna of the Flemish mystics, whose treatises of
regulated prayer he became acquainted with, we are told,
during his stay at Montserrat; further, occasionally, when for
example Ignatius recommends praying in rhythm by joining
a word of the *Pater Noster* to each breath, his method is
reminiscent of certain techniques of the Eastern Church (the
hesychasm of John Climaque, or continuous prayer linked to
respiration), to say nothing of course about the disciplines
of Buddhist meditation; however, these methods (to stay with
those Ignatius could have known) were aimed solely at
achieving within oneself an intimate theosophany, a union
with God. Ignatius gives the method of prayer a wholly different aim: it is a matter of the technical elaboration of an interlocution, i.e., a new language that can circulate between the
Divinity and the exercitant. The model of the task of prayer

here is much less mystical than rhetorical, for rhetoric was also the search for a second code, an artificial language, elaborated on the basis of a given idiom; the ancient orator disposed of rules (of selection and succession) for finding, assembling, and constructing arguments designed to reach the interlocutor and obtain from him a response; in the same way, Ignatius constitutes an "art" designed to determine divine interlocution. In both cases, general rules must be set down which can enable the subject to find what to say (*invenire quid dicas*), i.e., simply to speak: certainly at the outset of rhetoric and Ignatian meditation (whose minute detail we shall see, as though at each minute it were necessary to react against a speech inertia) there is the awareness of human aphasia: the orator and the exercitant, at the beginning, flounder in the profound deficiency of speech, as though they had nothing to say and that a strenuous effort were necessary to assist them in finding a language. It is doubtless for this reason that the methodological apparatus established by Ignatius, regulating days, schedules, postures, diets, makes us think in its extreme attention to detail of the writer's ceremonies (in general little known, it is true, and a pity): he who writes, by a regulated preparation of the material conditions for writing (place, schedule, notebooks, paper, etc.), what is commonly called the "labor" of the writer and which is most usually no more than the magic conjuration of his native aphasia, attempts to capture the "idea" (in which the rhetor assisted him), just as Ignatius is trying to provide the means for capturing the sign of Divinity.

The language Ignatius is trying to constitute is a language of interrogation. Whereas in natural idioms, the elementary structure of the sentence, articulated in subject and predicate, is assertive in order, the articulation current here is that of a question and an answer. This interrogative structure gives the *Exercises* its historical originality; hitherto, a commentator remarks, the preoccupation was more with carrying out God's will; Ignatius wants rather to discover this will (What is it? Where is it? Toward what does it tend?) and thereby his work joins a problematics of sign and not of perfection: the area of the *Exercises* is essentially that of the exchanged sign. Established between the Divinity and man, this area was, in the time of the ancient Greeks, that of mantic art, the art of divine consultation. A language of interpellation, mantic art is comprised of two codes: that of the question addressed by man to the Divinity, that of the response sent by the Divinity to man. Ignatian mantic art also comprises two codes; the first (or code of demand) is found mainly in the *Exercises,* the second (or code of response) in the *Journal;* however, as we shall see later, they cannot be disassociated; they are two correlative systems, a whole whose radically binary character attests its linguistic nature.

This can be ascertained merely by glancing at the over-all structure of the *Exercises.* Bizarre arguments have been advanced concerning this structure: it was not clear how Ignatius's four Weeks could coincide (since it was felt that they should) with the three paths (purgative, illuminative, unitive) of classical theology. How can 3 equal 4? This was got round by fractioning the second path into two parts, corresponding to the two median weeks. The stake of this taxinomic debate is in no way formal. The tripartite schema into which the four Weeks were to be made to fit covers the ordinary model of the rhetorical *disposito* which separates, in discourse, a beginning, a middle, and an end, or that of the syllogism, with its two premises and its conclusion; it is a dialectical schema (based on a notion of maturation), by which every process is naturalized, rationalized, acclimatized, pacified: to give the *Exercises* a tripartite structure is to reconcile the retreatant, to lend him the consolation of a mediatized transformation. However, no theological motive can prevail against this structural evidence: the number 4 (since there are four Weeks of retreat) refers, without any possible transaction, to a binary figure. As one of the most recent commentators of Ignatius has indicated,[2] the four Weeks are articulated into two moments, a *before* and an *after;* the pivot of this duality, which is not at all a "middle space" but a center, is, at the end of the second Week, the free act by which the exercitant chooses, in conformity with the Divine will, this or that conduct about which he has previously been uncertain: what Ignatius calls *to elect.* Election is not a dialectical moment, it is the abrupt contact of a freedom and a will; *before,* the conditions of a good election; *after,* the consequences; in the middle, freedom, i.e., substantially, nothing

The election (the choice) uses up the over-all function of the *Exercises.* The text having become sweetened by time, the *Exercises* has now and then been given a vague role of pious edification; Père Clément, an eighteenth-century translator, twists the *Exercises* and attributes to each Week, as if to an independent organ, an amovable function: for a good confession, the first Week, for an important decision, the second; for a troubled religious soul, the last two. Yet, linked to a unique structure, the function of the *Exercises* cannot but be unique: as in any mantic art, it is to determine a choice, a decision. This choice can undoubtedly be given theological generality (How unite on all occasions my freedom with the will of the Eternal?); however, the *Exercises* is very material, imbued with a spirit of contingency (which gives it its force and flavor); the choice it prepares and sanctions is truly practical. Ignatius has himself given a sample of the matters upon which an election is called for: priesthood, marriage, benefices, the way to direct a religious house, how much to give to the poor, etc. The best example of election, however, is not given in the *Exercises,* but in the *Spiritual Journal:* there, Ignatius dwells on the question which he has for several

---

[2] G. Fessard, *La Dialectique des Exercices spirituels de saint Ignace de Loyola* (Paris: Aubier, 1956).

months been attempting to answer within himself, soliciting God for a determining sign: in the Constitution of the Society of Jesus, should the churches be allowed the right to have revenues? There comes a moment in the deliberation where it is *yes* or *no,* and it is at this extreme point of choice that God's response must come. Also, the language of interrogation developed by Ignatius is aimed less at the classical question of consultations: *What to do?* than at the dramatic alternative by which finally every practice is prepared and determined: *To do this or to do that?* For Ignatius, every human act is by nature paradigmatic. Now, for Aristotle too: *praxis* is a science, and this science rests on an approximately alternative operation, *proairesis,* which consists in disposing points of bifurcation in the project of a line of conduct, in examining both perspectives, in choosing one and not the other, and then in moving on. This is the very moment of election, and we can see what can link *praxis* and the language of interrogation: what they share is the strictly binary form: the duality of every practical situation corresponds to the duality of a language articulated in demand and response. Consequently, we can better understand the originality of this third text of the *Exercises,* of this code Ignatius has instituted to bring God to bear upon the *praxis:* ordinarily, codes are invented to be deciphered; this one is invented for deciphering (the will of God).

Imagination

The invention of a language, this then is the object of the *Exercises.* This invention is prepared for by a certain number of protocols, which can be assembled under a unique prescription of isolation: retreat in a place shut away, solitary, and above all unaccustomed, lighting conditions (adapted to the subject of the meditation), dispositions of the room where the exercitant is to stay, positions (kneeling, prostrate, standing, sitting, gazing upward), facial expression, which must be restrained, and above all, of course, the organization of time, completely governed by the code, from waking to sleeping, including the day's most ordinary occupations (dressing, eating, lying down, sleeping). These prescriptions are not confined to Ignatius's system, they can be found in the economy of all religions, but in Ignatius they have the special quality of preparing the exercise of a language. How? By helping to determine what might be called a field of exclusion. The tight organization of time, for example, allows for the day to be completely *covered,* to cover over any interstice in it through which an outside word might come; to be repellent, the day must be joined together so perfectly that Ignatius recommends beginning the future tense even before the present tense has been exhausted: in going to sleep, think already of my awakening, in dressing, think of the exercise I am going to perform: an incessant *already* marks the retreatant's time and assures him a plenitude that removes far away from him any *other* language. The same function, albeit more indirect, for gestures: it is the prescription itself, not its content, that isolates; in its absurdity it deconditions the habitual, separates the exercitant from his anterior (different) gestures, removes the interference from the worldly tongues he spoke before entering the retreat (what Ignatius calls "indolent words"). All these protocols have the function of creating in the exercitant a kind of linguistic vacuum necessary for the elaboration and for the triumph of the new language: the vacuum is ideally the anterior space of all semiophany.

It is in this negative, repellent sense that—at least at the outset—the Ignatian imagination must be interpreted. Here, a distinction must be made between the image reservoir and the imagination. The image reservoir can be conceived as a body of interior representations (the common meaning) or as an image's field of eclipse (the meaning found in Bachelard and in thematic criticism), or even as the subject's misappre-

hension of himself at the moment he assumes stating and ful-
filling his *I* (J. Lacan's meaning of the word). Now, the image
reservoir of Ignatius is very poor in all these meanings. The
network of images he spontaneously draws upon (or which
he lends to the exercitant) is nearly nonexistent, to the point
that precisely all the labor of the *Exercises* consists in providing images to one who is innately without them; produced
with great difficulty, through strenuous technique, these
images are still banal, skeletal: if hell is to be "imagined," it
will be (the memories of a wise imagery) fires, screams, sulfur, tears; nowhere these journeys of transformation, these
"dream avenues" out of which Bachelard was able to construct his thematics, never, in Ignatius, one of these substan-
tial singularities, these material surprises to be found in
Ruysbroeck[3] or John of the Cross; for a description of the
thing imagined, Ignatius very quickly substitutes an intellectual cipher: yes, Lucifer is seated in a kind of "huge chariot
of fire and smoke," but for the rest, his aspect is merely "horrible and terrifying." As for the Ignatian *I,* at least in the
Exercises, it has no value in existence, it is not described,

[3] Here, a vision of hell in Ruysbroeck: "The gluttons will be fed on
sulfur and boiling pitch. . . . The fire they shall swallow will give
them internal sweating. . . . Were your body of bronze and a drop
of this sweat were to fall upon you, you would melt. I recall a horrible
example. Three monks lived near the Rhine, addicted to this hideous
passion. Disdaining the brothers' meal, they left the community at
mealtime to eat alone and in secret what they had prepared for themselves exclusively. Two of them suddenly died. One of the dead appeared to the survivor and said he was damned. Do you suffer much?
asked he who was still alive. In answer, the dead man stretched out
his hand and let fall a drop of sweat onto the brass candelabra. The
candelabra melted in less than a second, like wax in a glowing
oven. . . ." (Ruysbroeck, *Oeuvres choisies,* translated by E. Hello
[Paris: Poussielgue, 1869], p. 148.) The important thing here is to
have imagined not the heat of hell, but the sweat of the damned, and
the sweat, not watery in substance, but corrosive, so that it is the
very opposite of the infernal fire, liquid, which is its surest agent.

51 | Loyola

predicated, its mention is purely transitive, imperative ("As soon as I awaken, I recall myself to mind . . . ," "to control my eyes," "to deprive myself of all light," etc.); this is the *shifter* ideally described by linguists, whose psychological vacuum, whose pure locutory existence ensures a kind of errancy through indefinite persons. In a word, in Ignatius, nothing resembling a reservoir of images, if it is not rhetorical.

As Ignatius's image reservoir is nonexistent, so his imagination is powerful (exhaustively cultivated). Understood by this word, which we shall use in the wholly active meaning it can have in Latin, is the energy which enables the fabrication of a language whose units will of course be "imitations," but not the images formed and stored up somewhere within the individual. As voluntary action, speech energy, production of a formal system of signs, the Ignatian imagination thus can and must have an apotropaic function; it is first and foremost the power of repulsing foreign images; like the structural rules of a language—which are not normative rules—it forms an *ars obligatoria* that determines less what has to be imagined than what it is not possible to imagine—or what it is impossible not to imagine.

This negative power is what must first be recognized in the fundamental act of meditation, which is concentration: to "contemplate," "fix," "see myself as through my imagination," "to see through the eyes of the imagination," "to place myself before the object," is first to eliminate, even to eliminate continuously, as though, contrary to appearances, mental fixation on an object could never be the basis of a positive emphasis, but only the permanent residue of a series of active, vigilant exclusions: the purity, the solitude of the image is its very being, to the point that Ignatius determines, as its most difficult attribute, the time during which it must last (the length of three *Pater Noster*'s, three *Ave Maria*'s, etc.). A slightly different form of this law of exclusion is the obligation placed upon the exercitant, on the one hand to keep all the physiological senses (sight, smell, etc.) occupied by successively aiming them toward the same object, and on the other to bring all the insignificant details of his daily life together into the unique language he must speak and whose code Ignatius is attempting to establish: thus the temporal needs from which he cannot escape, light, the weather outside, food, dress, which must be made "profitable" in order that they may be turned into image objects ("During meals, consider Christ our Lord as though one saw Him eating with His Disciples, His way of drinking, of looking, of speaking; and try to imitate Him"), following a kind of totalitarian economy in which everything, from the accidental to the futile and trivial, must be utilized: like the novelist, the exercitant is "someone for whom nothing is lost" (Henry James). All these preparatory protocols, by eliminating from the field of the retreat worldly, idle, physical, natural language, in short *other* languages, are aimed at achieving the homogeneity of the language to be constructed, in a word, its pertinence; they correspond to that *speech situation* which is not interior to the code (which is why linguists have barely studied it until now), but without which the constitutive ambiguity of the language would reach an intolerable threshold.

Articulation

Whoever reads the *Exercises* sees at first glance that the material is subjected to an incessant, painstaking, and almost obsessive separation; or more exactly, the *Exercises* is this separation itself, to which nothing is pre-existent: everything is immediately divided, subdivided, classified, numbered off in annotations, meditations, Weeks, points, exercises, mysteries, etc. A simple operation which myth attributes to the Creator of the world, separating day, night, man, woman, elements, and species, forms the continuing basis of Ignatian discourse: *articulation*. The concept has, in Ignatius, another name which recurs constantly throughout his work: *discern-*

ment: to discern is to distinguish, to separate, to part, to limit, to enumerate, to evaluate, to recognize the founding function of difference; *discretio,* an Ignatian word *par excellence,* designates a gesture so original that it can be applied to behavior (in the case of Aristotelian *praxis*) and judgments (the *discreta caritas,* clairvoyant charity, which knows in order to distinguish), as well as to discourses: *discretio* is the basis of all language, since everything linguistic is articulated.

The mystics understood it: the fascination and distrust they felt with regard to language are expressed in a heated debate on the discontinuity of inner experience: this is the problem of "distinct apprehensions."[4] Even when the goal of mystical experience is defined as being beyond language, where its very mark—which is the existence of articulated units—is obliterated, anterior states are classified, an inaugural language is described: Theresa of Avila discerns meditation, union, ecstasy, etc., and John of the Cross, who has certainly gone further than Theresa in obliterating the discontinuous, sets up a scrupulous code of apprehensions (exterior-bodily, interior-bodily, distinct and particular, confused, obscure, general, etc.). Articulation appears to all as the condition, warranty, and fate of language: to outstrip language, articulation must be exhausted, extenuated, after having been recognized. We know that this is not Ignatius's goal: the theophany he is methodically seeking is in fact a semiophany, what he is striving to obtain is more the sign of God than knowledge of Him or His presence; language is his definitive horizon and articulation an operation he can never abandon in favor of indistinct—ineffable—states.

The units Ignatius outlines are many. Some are temporal: weeks, days, moments, times. Others are oratorical: exercises,

---

[4] See Jean Baruzi, *Saint Jean de la Croix et le problème de l'expérience mystique* (Paris: Félix Alcan, 1924).

contemplations, meditations (essentially discursive in nature), tests, colloquia, preambles, prayers. Others, finally, are, one might say, merely metalinguistic: annotations, additions, points, manners, notes. This variety of distinctions (obviously on a scholastic model) results, as we have seen, from the need to occupy the totality of the mental territory and consequently to utilize to the extreme the channels through which speech energy will recover and so to speak color the exercitant's request. What is to be transported along this varied network of the *distinguo* is a unique material: the image. The image is very precisely a unit of imitation; the imitable material (principally the life of Christ) is divided into fragments so that it can be contained within a framework and fill it completely; the glowing bodies of hell, the screams of the damned, the acrid taste of tears, the persons of the Nativity, those of the Last Supper, the angel Gabriel's salutation to the Virgin, etc., so many image units (or "points"). This unit is not immediately anecdotal; alone, it does not necessarily make up a complete scene, mobilizing as in the theater several senses at one time: the image (imitation) can be purely visual, or purely auditory, or purely tactile, etc. What distinguishes it is its capability of being enclosed in a homogeneous field, or, better, framed: however, the frame Ignatius provides for it, derived in general from the rhetorical or psychological categories of the period (the five senses, the three powers of the soul, characters, etc.), is the willed product of a code, it has little relation to this fascination for the isolated object, the solitary and encircled detail which ecstasy imprints on the mystic or hallucinating conscience: thus, Theresa, suddenly receiving a vision of Christ's hands "of so marvelous a beauty that I am powerless to picture them," or the hashish eater impelled to lose himself for hours, according to Baudelaire, in contemplation of a bluish smoke ring. The Ignatian image is separated only insofar as it is articulated: what constitutes it is its being caught up simultaneously in a difference and a contiguity (of the narrative type); thus it is contrasted with the "vision" (which Ignatius had experienced and on which he reports in his *Journal*), indistinct, elementary, and above all erratic ("felt or saw very luminously the Divine Being or Essence itself in the form of a sphere a little larger than the sun"). The Ignatian image is not a *vision,* it is a *view,* in the sense this word has in graphic art (View of Naples, View from the Pont-au-Change, etc.); again, this "view" must be captured in a narrative sequence, somewhat after the fashion of Carpaccio's St. Ursula, or the successive illustrations in a novel.

These views (stretching the meaning of the word, since it entails all the units of image-reservoir perception) can "frame" tastes, odors, sounds, or feelings, but it is the "visual" sight, one might say, which receives all of Ignatius's attention. Its subjects are various: a temple, a mountain, a vale of tears, the Virgin's chamber, a warrior camp, a garden, a sepulcher, etc.; its detail is painstaking (consider the length of the road, its width, if it passes through a plain or across valleys and hills, etc.). These views, whose suggestion in principle precedes every exercise, are the famous *composición viendo el lugar.* The composition of place was supported by a dual tradition. First, a rhetorical tradition; the second, sophistic or neo-rhetorical Alexandrine, had consecrated place description under the name *topography;* Cicero recommended, when speaking of a place, considering whether it was flat, mountainous, harmonious, rough, etc. (exactly what Ignatius says); and Aristotle, stating that in order to remember things one must recognize where they are, includes place (*topos*), common or particular, in his rhetoric of the probable; in Ignatius, place, material as it may be, has this logical function: it has an associative force which Ignatius attempts to exploit. Next, a Christian tradition, going back to the High Middle Ages; a tradition ignored by Theresa of Avila, incapable as she said of exercising her imagination on given places, but which Ignatius systematized, to the point of wanting at the end of his life to publish a book in which compositions of place would have been illustrated with engravings (Father Jerome Nadal was entrusted with preparing a volume of prints of Gospel scenes coded by the *Exercises,* and in the eighteenth century, Ignatius's manual was abundantly illustrated). Finally, we shall see that the exceptional, and exceptionally systematized, scope Ignatius gives to the language of "views" has a historical and so to speak dogmatic significance; however, the prime originality of this language is semiological: Ignatius has linked the image to an order of discontinuity, he has articulated imitation, and he has thus made the image a linguistic unit, the element of a code.

The Tree

The articulation with which the image is stamped divides a contiguity; it is syntagmatic in nature and corresponds to that opposition of units within a sentence which linguists call "contrast." Ignatian language also contains the rough outline of a system of virtual or paradigmatic oppositions. Ignatius stubbornly practices this exasperated form of binarism, the antithesis: for example, the whole of the second Week is regulated by the opposition of two reigns, two standards, two camps, that of Christ and that of Lucifer, whose attributes counter each other one to one; every sign of excellence unerringly determines the mold where it structurally takes support in order to signify: the wisdom of God and my ignorance, His omnipotence and my weakness, His justice and my iniquity, His goodness and my evil, all paradigmatic couplings. Jakobson, as we know, has defined the "poetic" as the actualization and extension of a systematic opposition, on the plan of the spoken chain; Ignatian discourse is made up of these extensions which, were they graphically projected, would have the appearance of a network of knots and branchings; a relatively simple network when the branchings are bifurcations (in the fourteenth and fifteenth centuries, the implied choice in a matter of conscience was called *binary*), but which can grow extremely complicated when the branchings are multiple. The development of the discourse then resembles the spreading of a tree, a well-known figure among linguists. Here, sketched out, is the tree of the first Week:

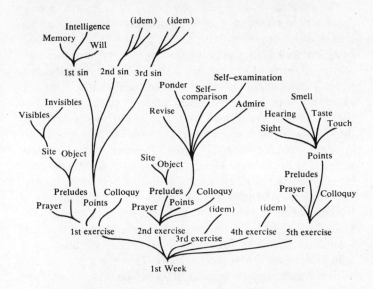

It is useful to picture the continuous arborescence of Ignatian discourse, for then we can see it open out like an organigram designed to regulate the transformation of a request into language, or: the production of a number capable of exciting the Divinity's reply. The *Exercises* is somehow machine-like, in the cybernetic sense of the term: a raw "case" is fed in, which is the material of election; it should give back not, of course, an automatic response, but a coded and thereby "acceptable" (in the sense this word can have in linguistics) request. We shall see that the Ignatian tree has the paradoxical purpose of *equilibrating* the elements of choice and not, as one might have expected, of preferring one of them; for what is coded is the appeal for God's sign, but not directly that sign itself.

Topics

The Ignatian tree suggests the notion of a growth, a conducting of the request (object of the Exercise) through an interlacing of branches: however, to be subdivided, the theme being subjected to meditation needs a supplementary apparatus to furnish its gamut of possibilities; this apparatus is a topic. The topic, an important part of the *inventio,* a reserve of common or particular sites, whence could be derived the premise for the enthymemes, has had great good fortune throughout all of ancient rhetoric. "Region of arguments," "circle," "sphere," "source," "well," "arsenal," "hive," "treasure house of dormant ideas," rhetors have incessantly celebrated it as the absolute means of having something to say. A form pre-existent to any invention, the topic is a grill, a tablature of cases through which the subject to be treated (the *questio*) is guided: this methodical contact produces the idea —or at least its inception, which the syllogism will be charged with prolonging almost mechanically. Thus the topic contains all the wonders of an arsenal of latent powers. There have been many topics, from the purely formal topic of Aristotle to the "responsive topic" of Vico; and it can be said that even after its death, many discourses have carried on the process without taking the name.

The profit Ignatius was able to derive from this tool can be imagined: the subject of meditation (always posited in the form of a request of God in one of the preambles to the Exercise) is methodically confronted, point by point, with the items on a list, so as to evoke the images with which Ignatius is composing his language. The lists of Ignatius (the topics) are, principally: the Ten Commandments, the Seven

Deadly Sins, the three powers of the soul (memory, understanding, will), and above all the five senses; thus the imagining of Hell consists in perceiving it five consecutive times in
the mode of each of the five senses: seeing the incandescent
bodies, hearing the screams of the damned, smelling the stink
of the abyss, tasting the bitterness of tears, touching the fire.
More: as the subject itself can subdivide itself into particular
points and as it is required to pass each of these points along
all the cases of the topic, so the exercitant must undertake a
veritable weaving of meditation, the points of the subject furnishing the woof and the cases of the topic the warp; thus,
each of the three sins, that of the Angels, that of Adam, and
that of man, must be thrice traversed, along the three avenues
of memory, understanding and will. Here too the law of totalitarian economy which has already been mentioned takes
effect: everything is covered over, blanketed, exhausted.

Ignatius even imagines a free topic, close to the association
of ideas: the second manner of prayer consists in "contemplating the word *Pater*. One will continue to consider this
word as long as one can find meanings, comparisons, taste
and consolation in the considerations bound up in this word";
an hour can thus be spent on the *Pater Noster* as a whole.
This is a very widespread technique: it is a method of concentration familiar in the Middle Ages under the name *Lectio
divina* and in Buddhism as *nembutsu* or meditation on the
name of Buddha. Gracian has given a baroque, more literary
version, which consists in breaking the name down into its
etymological albeit whimsical components (*Di-os,* he who has
given us life, fortune, our children, etc.): this is the *agudeza
nominal,* a kind of rhetorical *annominatio*. But whereas for
the Buddhist nominal concentration should produce a vacuum, Ignatius recommends an exploration of all the signifieds
of a single noun in order to arrive at a whole; he wants to
wrest from the form the whole gamut of its meanings and
thereby extenuate the subject—this subject which in our

terminology is endowed with a pleasing ambiguity, since it is simultaneously *quaestio* and *ego,* object and agent of the discourse.

Assemblages

What has been articulated must be reassembled. The exercitant's text contains two major forms of assemblage, repetition and narrative.

Repetition is a principal element in the pedagogy of the *Exercises.* First, there is a literal repetition, which is redoing an Exercise completely in its progression and in its details; this is *rumination* (Ignatius's word). Next there is recapitulation, the old classical schema of *summatio,* frequently used over the centuries: on the seventh day of the third Week, Ignatius thus recommends taking up and considering the Passion as a whole. Lastly, there is varied repetition, consisting in taking a subject and changing its viewpoint; if, for example, on the point of an election, I stop to think about my choice, I must consider what the results of this choice will be on the day of my death, and on the day of the Last Judgment. Repetition consists in exhausting the "pertinences" of a subject: one repeats, varying a little bit, in order to be sure of covering everything. The complex model of Ignatian repetition could well be the fourfold formula which is said to sum up the four Weeks of the *Exercises:* (1) *Deformata reformare,* (2) *Reformata conformare,* (3) *Conformata confirmare,* (4) *Confirmata transformare;* with two roots and four prefixes, everything is not only uttered but even repeated, like a whole whose individual parts slightly overlap in order to ensure a perfect join. Ignatian repetition is not mechanical, it has a closing, or more exactly a staggering, function: the repeated fragments are like the walls—or the notched joints—of a redan.

The second form of assemblage is the narrative. This must

be understood, in the formal sense, as being any discourse
having a structure the terms of which are differentiated, relatively free (open to alternative and therefore to suspense),
reductive (the résumé), and expandable (secondary elements
can be infinitely intercalated). The meditations Ignatius elab-
orates from an excerpting of the Gospel narrative, whose
episodes are presented at the conclusion of the *Exercises* as
mysteries, possess these characteristics; they can be summarized (the résumé is generally given in one of the preambles: the *history,* the Ciceroninan *narratio,* the exposition
of facts, *rerum explicatio,* the first deployment of the thing);
they can also be augmented, dilated, as Ignatius expressly indicates; finally, they have the pathetic attribute of narrative
structure: suspense; for although the story of Christ is known
and contains no anecdotal surprise, it is still possible to
dramatize its repercussions by reproducing in oneself the form
of suspense, making the belated or uncertain shadow disappear; when he recites the Life of Christ, the exercitant must
not hurry, he must exhaust each Station, do each Exercise
without reference to its successor, not allow to arise to soon,
out of order, the emotions of consolatior, in short, he must
respect the suspense of feelings, if not of facts. By virtue of
this narrative structure, the "mysteries" excerpted by Ignatius
from the Christian narrative take on a theatrical quality which
relates them to the medieval mysteries: they are "scenes" the
exercitant is called upon to live out, as in a psychodrama.

The exercitant is in fact called upon to invest himself in the
narrative as well as in the repetition. He is to repeat what de-
presses, consoles, traumatizes, enraptures him in each narrative; he is to live the anecdote by identifying himself with
Christ: "To demand sorrow with the sorrowing Christ, lacera-
tion with the lacerated Christ." The Exercise basically implies a *pleasure* (in the ambiguous meaning we can today see
in that word), and the Ignatian theater is less rhetorical than
fantasmatic: its "scene" is in fact a "scenario."

Fantasm

"The *Exercises*," says a Jesuit commentator,[5] "is an area at once formidable and desirable . . ." Indeed, anyone reading the *Exercises* cannot help but be struck by the mass of desire which agitates it. The immediate force of this desire is to be read in the very materiality of the objects whose representation Ignatius calls for: places in their precise, complete dimensions, characters in their costumes, their attitudes, their actions, their actual words. The most abstract things (which Ignatius calls "invisibles") must find some material movement where they can picture themselves and form a *tableau vivant*: if the Trinity is to be envisioned, it will be in the form of three Persons in the act of watching men descending into hell; however, the basis, the force of the materiality, the immediate total of desire, is of course the human body; a body incessantly mobilized into image by the play of imitation which establishes a literal analogy between the corporeality of the exercitant and that of Christ, whose existence, almost physiological, is to be rediscovered through personal anamnesis. The body in Ignatius is never conceptual: it is always *this* body: if I transport myself to a vale of tears, I must imagine, see *this* flesh, *these* members among the bodies of the creatures, and perceive the infection emanating from this mysterious object, the demonstrative of which (*this* body) exhausts the situation, since it can never be defined, only designated. The body's deictism is reinforced by the way it is transmitted, the image. The image is in fact by nature deictic, it designates, it does not define; it always contains a residue of contingency, which can merely be indicated. Semiologically, the image always sweeps on beyond the signified toward the pure materiality of the referent. Ignatius always follows this flow, which attempts to found meaning on matter and not on concept; placing himself before the Cross (placing that body before the Cross),

[5] F. Courel, Introduction to *Exercices spirituels* (Paris: Desclée de Brouwer, 1960).

he attempts to go beyond the signified of the image (the Christian, universally meditated meaning) to its referent, the material Cross, this crossed wood whose circumstantial attributes he attempts, through the imagining senses, to perceive. This upward movement toward matter, which forms the essential part of the devout realism whose "revolting crudity" Renan deplored, is conducted in the manner of a conscious fantasy, a controlled improvisation (is this not the musical and Freudian meaning of *phantasieren?*): in the isolated and darkened room in which one meditates, everything is prepared for the fantastic meeting of desire, formed by the material body, and of the "scene" drawn from allegories of desolation and the Gospel mysteries.

For this theater is entirely created in order that the exercitant may therein represent himself: his body is what is to occupy it. The very development of the retreat, throughout the final three Weeks, follows the story of Christ: he is born with Him, travels with Him, eats with Him, undergoes the Passion with Him. The exercitant is continually required to imitate twice, to imitate what he imagines: to think of Christ "as though one saw Him eating with His disciples, His way of drinking, of looking, of speaking; and try to imitate Him." The Christomorphic theme always fascinated Ignatius: studying in Paris and seeking employment with a form master in a college, "he imagined his master was Christ, that to one of the students he gave the name St. Peter and to another St. John . . . and when the master gives me an order, I will think that it is Christ who has given it."[6] Deiform (in Ruysbroeck's word) existence provides the scene, anecdotal matter the fantasy; in the latter, we know, by definition, the subject must be present:[7] *someone* real (Ignatius, the exercitant, the

[6] *Récit du Pèlerin* (Paris: Desclée de Brouwer, 1956), p. 112.

[7] The fantasy is "an imaginary scenario in which the subject is present and which embodies . . . the fulfillment of a desire" (Laplanche and Pontalis, *Dictionnaire de Psychanalyse* [Paris: Presses Universitaires de France, 1967]).

reader, whoever) takes his place and his part in the scene: the *I* appears: "Imagining Christ our Lord before me, placed upon the Cross, speaking with Him," etc.; before the actors in the Nativity, "make myself a poor man or a worthless slave who looks upon Them, contemplates Them and serves Their needs, as though I myself were present"; "I am a knight humbled before an entire court, and before his king";[8] "I am a sinner in chains before his judge," etc. This *I* takes advantage of all the situations the Gospel canvas provides in order to fulfill the symbolic motions of desire: humiliation, jubilation, fear, effusion, etc. It has absolute plasticity: it can transform itself, reduce itself according to the needs of the comparison—"Consider who I am and make myself smaller and smaller through comparisons with (a) other men, (b) the Angels, (c) God." As in the hashish dream, whose alternately reductive and expansive effect Baudelaire describes, the Ignatian *I,* when it imagines in a fantasizing manner, is not a person; Ignatius can here and there, anecdotally, assign it a place in the scene; fantasmatically, however, the situation is fluid, dispersed; the exercitant (supposing him to be the subject of the meditation) does not disappear but displaces himself in the thing, like the hashish smoker totally caught up in the smoke from his pipe, who "smokes himself": he is no more than the verb that sustains and justifies the scene. It is certainly not from such a viewpoint that the famous sentence attributed to Ignatius (in fact, it comes from an *Elogium sepulcrale S. Ignatii*) was written: *"Non coerceri maximo, contineri tamen a minimo, divinum est"* (Not to be encompassed by the greatest, but to be contained by the smallest, is a divine thing); however, we have only to recall the sympathy with which Hölderlin quoted it to see it as the

[8] Desirous of "adapting" the Ignatian allegory of the temporal king "to the spirit of our own time," the Jesuit Coathalem suggests substituting for the divine-right king in the scenario of the humiliating compearance, "some great leader of industry with outstanding talents"!

motto for that evasive presence of the subject within the image which marks both fantasm and Ignatian contemplation.

The Orthodoxy of the Image

At the beginning of the modern era, in Ignatius's century, one fact seems to begin to modify the exercise of the imagination: a reordering of the hierarchy of the five senses. In the Middle Ages, historians tell us, the most refined sense, the perceptive sense *par excellence,* the one that established the richest contact with the world, was hearing: sight came in only third place, after touch. Then we have a reversal: the eye becomes the prime organ of perception (Baroque, art of the thing seen, attests to it). This change is of great religious importance. The primacy of hearing, still very prevalent in the sixteenth century, was theologically guaranteed: the Church bases its authority on the word, faith is hearing: *auditum verbi Dei, id est fidem;* the ear, the ear alone, Luther said, is the Christian organ. Thus a risk of a contradiction arises between the new perception, led by sight, and the ancient faith based on hearing. Ignatius sets out, as a matter of fact, to resolve it: he attempts to situate the image (or interior "sight") in orthodoxy, as a new unit of the language he is constructing.

Yet there are religious oppositions to the image (aside from the auditory mark of faith, received, upheld, and reaffirmed by the Reformation). The first are ascetic in origin; sight, the procuress of touch, is easily associated with desire of the flesh (although the antique myth of sedution was that of the Sirens, i.e., melodic temptation), and the ascetic shunned it all the more so in that it is impossible to live without seeing; further, one of the predecessors of John of the Cross imposed a five-foot limit on his visual perception, beyond which he was not to look. Anterior to language ("Before language," Bonald says, "there was nothing but bodies and their images"), the image was thought to represent something barbaric and, in a word, "natural," which rendered it suspect to any disciplinary morality. Perhaps this mistrust vis-à-vis the image represents the presentiment that sight is closer to the unconscious and all that animates it, as Freud has noted. The Church developed additional, more ambiguous oppositions to the image: those of the mystics. Commonly, images (particularly visions and, with greater reason, "sight," of an inferior order) are not admitted in mystical experience save in a preparatory role: they are exercises for debutants; for John of the Cross, images, forms and meditations are suitable only for beginners. The goal of the experience is, on the contrary, the deprivation of images; it is to "mount with Jesus to the summit of our spirit, on the mountain of Nakedness, without image" (Ruysbroeck). John of the Cross notes that the soul "in an act of confused, amorous, peaceful, and fulfilled ideation" (successful in relinquishing distinct images) cannot without painful fatigue return to particular contemplations, in which one discourses in images and forms; and Theresa of Avila, although in this respect she occupies an intermediate position between John of the Cross and Ignatius Loyola, keeps aloof when it comes to the imagination: "So inert is this faculty in me that despite all my efforts I can never picture or represent to myself the Holy Humanity of our Lord (a representation which Ignatius, as we have seen, incessantly provokes, varies, and exploits). It is well known that from a mystical viewpoint, abyssal faith is dark, submerged, flowing (says Ruysbroeck) in the immense shadow of God Who is the "face of sublime nothingness," meditations, contemplations, visions, sights, and discourses, in short, images, occupying only the "spirit's husk."

We know that to these mistrustings of the image Ignatius responded with a radical imperialism of the image: product of the guided imagination, the image is the abiding material of the *Exercises:* the sights, representations, allegories, mysteries (or Gospel anecdotes) constantly created by the image-making senses are the constitutive units of meditation and, as has been said earlier, this figurative material quite naturally engendered, after Ignatius's death, a literature of illustrations, of engravings, that have sometimes been adapted to the countries whose evangelization they were intended to promote: some were presented to the last Ming emperor. The image, however, is not recognized, promoted, save by means of a systematic treatment of which Ignatius made himself the prime practitioner, and which is nowhere to be found in the condescending attitudes the mystics adopted toward visions, before abandoning them for the lone, divine shadow. Indeed, there is a way theologically to clear the image "through customs": that is to make it not the rung of a unitive ascent, but the unit of a language.

To constitute the field of the image as a linguistic system is in fact to forearm oneself against the suspect marginal zones of the mystical experience: language is the guarantor of orthodox faith doubtless (among other reasons) because it authenticates the specificity of the Christian confession. Language—in its expressly articulated nature—is precisely what Bossuet uses to oppose the Quietist heresy (whose historical relationships with John of the Cross are common knowledge): against Mme Guyon, who defined empty prayer as "a profound withdrawal, without act or discourse," Bossuet decreed that "the act of faith must manifest itself in a discursive manner, the soul must explicitly demand its well-being": in short, there is no prayer other than articulated. Articulation is what in fact Ignatius brings to the image, the path he takes to give it a linguistic being, and hence an orthodoxy. We have seen how this punctuation, which we know to be the condition necessary and proper to all language, reigns in the *Exercises,* cutting up, subdividing, bifurcating and trifurcating, combining every strictly semantic operation designed to combat relentlessly the vague and the empty.

The guarantees afforded by this image linguistics are of three orders. First, a realist guarantee: whereas, according to Merleau-Ponty, the hallucinated contains an implicit and

inarticulated significance, the true is "stuffed with tiny perceptions which bring it into existence": the images which
Ignatius outlines are not hallucinations, they are modeled
after the intelligible real. Next, a logical guarantee: the punctuation of images permits a gradual development, the same
rhythm as that of logical progressions. Buddhism has doctrines called (in Chinese) *torin,* wherein the opening up of
the spirit is a separate, sudden, abrupt, discontinuous (as in
Zen) event, and doctrines called *kien,* wherein this same illumination is the result of a gradual (but not continuous)
method. The *Exercises* is *kien,* more paradoxically so in that
the image commonly stands as the privileged basis for immediate intuition and abrupt rapture. Further, articulation
permits the predication of God; every mystical effort is taken
to reduce (or expand, as one will) God to His essence (Maimonides, through John of the Cross: "Concerning God, we
grasp nothing other than that *He is,* but not *What He is*"),
and this effort already contains within itself the condemnation of all language; choosing the path of an exasperated
punctuation, Ignatius opens to the Divinity a list, at once
metaphorical and metonymic, of its attributes; it is possible
to speak God. Lastly, an ethical guarantee: the speculative
mystic (John of the Cross, for example) is satisfied with
something beyond language; Ignatian discontinuity, the linguistic vocation of the *Exercises,* are on the contrary in conformity with the mystique of "service" practiced by Ignatius:
there is no *praxis* without code (we have mentioned this
apropos Aristotelian *proairesis*), but also, every code is a link
to the world: the energy of language (of which the *Exercises*
is one of the exemplary theaters) is a form—and the very
form of a desire of the world.

Accountancy

The *Exercises* can be conceived as a desperate struggle
against the dispersal of images which psychologically, they

say, marks mental experience and over which—every religion agrees—only an extremely rigorous method can triumph. Ignatian imagination, as has been stated, has first this function of selection and concentration: it is a matter of casting out these fleeting images that invade the spirit like "a disorderly swarm of flies" (Theophanes the Hermit) or "capricious monkeys leaping from branch to branch (Ramakrishna); but to substitute what for them? In fact, it is not against the proliferation of images that the *Exercises* is finally struggling, but, far more dramatically, against their inexistence, as though, originally emptied of fantasms, the exercitant (whatever the dispersion of his spirit) needed assistance in providing himself with them. It can be said that Ignatius takes as much trouble filling the spirit with images as the mystics (Christians and Buddhists) do in emptying them out; and if we turn to certain present-day hypotheses,[9] which define the psychosomatic patient as a subject powerless to produce fantasies and his cure as a methodical effort to bring him to a "capacity for fantasy manipulation," Ignatius is then a psychotherapist attempting at all costs to inject images into the dull, dry and empty spirit of the exercitant, to introduce into him this culture of fantasy, preferable despite the risks to that fundamental *nothingness* (nothing to say, to think, to imagine, to feel, to believe) which marks the subject of the speech before the rhetors or the Jesuits bring their technique to bear and give it a language. In short, the retreatant must be "made neurotic."

Obsessional neurosis has been defined (Lacan) as a "defensive decomposition comparable in its principles to that illustrative of the redan or the obstacle." This is precisely the structure of the *Exercises;* not only is the ascetic matter broken up, articulated in the extreme, but in addition it is

---

[9] P. Marty, M. de M'Uzan, C. David, *L'Investigation psychosomatique* (Paris: Presses Universitaires de France, 1963).

set out in a discursive system of annotations, notes, points, preambles, precautions, repetitions, reversals, and consolidations which form the strongest of defenses. The obsessional character of the *Exercises* blazes forth in the accounting passion transmitted to the exercitant: as soon as an object, intellectual or imaginary, appears, it is broken up, divided, numbered. The accountancy is obsessional not only because it is infinite, but above all because it engenders its own errors: being a matter of accounting for his sins (and we shall see that in this regard Ignatius has provided a graphic bookkeeping technique), the fact of accounting for them in a faulty way will in turn become an error that must be added on to the original list; this list is thus made infinite, the redeeming accounting of errors calling up *per contra* the very errors of the account: for example, the particular Examination for the first Week is above all designed to make an accounting of the lapses committed with regard to prayer. In fact, it is the neurotic nature of obsession to set up a self-maintaining machine, a kind of homeostat of error, constructed in such a way that its function alone provides it with operating energy; thus we see Ignatius, in his *Journal,* requesting a sign from God, God delaying in giving it, Ignatius growing impatient, accusing himself for being impatient, and recommencing the circuit: one prays, one regrets praying badly, one adds to the faulty prayer a supplementary prayer for forgiveness, etc.; or: in order to decide whether masses designed to inspire a good decision should be abandoned, one plans . . . to say another mass. Accountancy has a mechanical advantage: for being the language of a language, it is able to support an infinite circularity of errors and of their accounting. It has a further advantage: dealing with sins, it helps to create between the sinner and the countless number of his sins a narcissistic bond of property: lapse is a means of acceding to the individual's identity, and in this sense the totally bookkeeping nature of sin as Ignatius's manual establishes it and which was little known in the Middle Ages, aware, above all, it seems, in a more cosmic way of original sin and of hell, cannot be completely foreign to the new capitalist ideology, articulated both on the individualist awareness of the person and on the inventorying of the goods which, belonging to him personally, constitute him. We see the ambiguity of the *Exercises;* it establishes a psychotherapy designed to awaken, to make resonate, through the production of a fantasmatic language, the dullness of this body which has nothing to say, but at the same time it provokes a neurosis whose very obsession protects the submission of the retreatant (or Christian) with regard to the Divinity. In an other way it might be said that Ignatius (and the Church with him) sets up a psychotherapy for the exercitant, but constantly refuses to resolve the transferential relationship that it implies. A situation with which must be contrasted—if we want truly to understand the Christian particularity toward which we can be blinded through force of habit—another type of ascesis, Zen for example, whose entire effort is on the contrary to "de-obsessionalize" meditation by subverting, in order better to supersede them, classes, lists, enumerations—in short, articulation, or even: language itself.

The Scale and the Mark

To conclude, we must return to the multiple text of the *Exercises*. Everything we have hitherto said concerned above all the third text, the active text, by which the exercitant, in possession of the language of interrogation established for him by Ignatius, attempts to obtain from the Divinity a response to the practical dilemma of his actions, i.e., a "good choice." It remains to be seen what Ignatius has been able to say about the language of the Divinity, this second facet of every mantic art.

This language—it has been ever thus—reduced itself down to a unique sign, which is never more than the designation of one of the two terms of an alternative; this designation, which can be uttered in many ways, is the ancient *numen,* the nod by which the Divinity says *yes* or *no* to what is set before it. The rhetoric implied by the third text of the *Exercises* in fact consists in effacing the obstacles to deliberation, in reducing it obstacle by obstacle to an equal alternative where the sign from God can intervene simply. We see what the Divinity's role is: it is to *mark* one of the two terms of the binary. Now, this is the fundamental mechanism of every linguistic apparatus: a paradigm of two equal terms is given, one of the terms is marked against the other, which is not marked, and the meaning emerges, the message is uttered. In mantic art, the *numen* is the mark itself, its elementary state. This production of meaning is not devoid of reminders, on the lay level, of Platonic rhetoric, as it can be seen at work, for example, in the *Sophist:* for this rhetoric, too, it is a question of progressing in the discourse by a series of alternatives, the interlocutor being requested to mark one of the terms: it is the concession of the respondent, linked to the master by an amorous relationship, which removes the alternative from the impasse and permits proceeding to the next alternative, thereby coming ever closer to the essence of the thing. In mantic art, the divinity, faced with the alternative offered by the questioner, in like manner *concedes* one of the terms: that is its answer. In the Ignatian system, paradigms are given by the discernment, but only God can mark them: the generator of meaning, but not its preparer, He is, structurally, the Marker, he who imparts a difference.

This distribution of linguistic functions is a rigorous one. The exercitant's role is not to choose, i.e., to mark, but quite the contrary to offer for the divine mark a perfectly equal alternative. The exercitant must strive not to choose; the aim of his discourse is to bring the two terms of the alternative to a homogeneous state so pure that he cannot humanly extricate himself from it; the more equal the dilemma the more rigorous its closure, and the clearer the divine *numen,* or:

the more certain it will be that the mark is of divine origin; the more completely will the paradigm be balanced, and the more tangible will be the imbalance God will impart to it. This paradigmatic equality is the famous Ignatian *indifference* which has so outraged the Jesuit's foes: to will nothing oneself, to be as disposable as a corpse, *perinde ac cadaver;* one of Ignatius's disciples, Jerome Nadal, when asked what he had decided, replied that he was inclined toward nothing save to be inclined toward nothing. This indifference is a virtuality of possibles which one works to make equal in weight, as though one were to construct an extremely sensitive scale on which one would place materials constantly being brought into balance, so that the arm leans neither to one side nor to the other: it is the Ignatian *balance sheet:* "I must be indifferent, without any inordinate attachment, so as not to be either more inclined or attached to taking what is offered me than to leaving it, no more to leaving it than taking it. Yet I must be like the needle of a scale in order to follow what I feel to be more for the glory and praise of God our Lord and for the salvation of my soul."

Consequently, it is clear that measure here is not a mere rhetorical notion, but a structural value which has a very precise role in the linguistic system Ignatius has elaborated: it is the very condition that permits offering the best possible paradigm for marking. Measure guarantees the language itself, and here we find once again the contrast we have already noted between Ignatian ascesis and Flemish mysticism: for Ruysbroeck there is a link between the subversion of the very function of language and the vertigo of excess; contrasted with the strict accountancy instituted by Ignatius is the mystical intoxication ("I call intoxication of the spirit," Ruysbroeck says, "that state in which bliss surpasses the possibilities glimpsed by desire"), this intoxication so many hyperboles attempt to encompass ("the excess of transcendency," "the abyss of super-essence," "bliss crowned in measureless essence," "naked and super-essential beatitude"). A possible path of knowledge and union, excess cannot be a means of language; thus we see Ignatius struggle to preserve the purity of the milieu in which the scale is to operate ("Let the first rule of your actions be to act as though success depended upon you and not upon God, and to abandon yourself to God as though He were to do everything in your stead"[10]) and continually to re-establish the balance by appropriate calibrations: this is the technique of *contra agere,* which consists in systematically going in the direction opposite to that toward which the scale seems spontaneously to tip: "In order better to conquer every immoderate appetite and every temptation of the Foe, if one is tempted to eat more, let him eat less": excess is not corrected by a return to balance, but according to a more careful physics, by a countermeasure: an oscillating instrument, the scale does not come to rest in perfect balance save through the interplay of a *plus* and a *minus.*

Equality thus being achieved at the cost of a labor of which the *Exercises* forms the story, how will the Divinity, whose role it is, move the arm, mark one of the terms of the choice? The *Exercises* is the book of the question, not of the answer. In order to give some notion of the forms which the mark God puts on the scale can take, we must turn to the *Spiritual Journal;* there we shall find the outline of the divine code whose elements Ignatius notes down with the help of a whole repertoire of graphic signs which have not yet been completely deciphered (initials, dots, the // sign, etc.). These divine manifestations, as might be expected in an area dominated by the fantasmic, occur principally at the level of the body, this broken-up body whose fragmentation is precisely the path of fantasy. These are, first, tears; we are aware of the importance of the *gift of tears* in Christian history; for Ignatius, these very material tears (we are told that his dark eyes were always a bit veiled with weeping) constitute a veritable code whose matter is differentiated into signs according to the time of their

[10] Sentence attributed to Ignatius, but disputed.

appearance and their intensity.[11] Then follows the spontaneous flow of words, *loquency* (the nature of which is not, in
truth, very well known). There are also what might be called
coenesthetic sensations, diffused throughout the body, "produced in the soul by the Holy Spirit" (Ignatius calls them *de-
votions*), such as emotions of elevation, tranquillity, joy, feelings of heat, light, or proximity. Lastly, there are direct
theophanies: *visits* localized between "high" (the abode of the
Trinity) and "low" (the Missal, the formula) and *visions,*
numerous in Ignatius's life, which frequently occur to confirm
decisions taken.

Yet, despite their codification, none of these "motions" is,
directly, decisive. Thus we see Ignatius (in his *Journal,* where
it is a question of obtaining a reply from God relative to a
very precise point in the Jesuit Constitution) wait, watch the
motions, note them, account for them, persist in eliciting
them, and even become impatient when they do not succeed
in constituting an indubitable mark. There is but one outcome
to this dialogue in which the Divinity speaks (for the motions
are numerous) but does not mark: it is to make the withholding of the mark itself into an ultimate sign. This last lecture,
the final and difficult fruit of ascesis, is *respect,* the reverential
acceptance of God's silence, the assent given not to the sign,
but to the sign's delay. Hearing turns into its own answer,
and from being suspensive, the interrogation becomes somehow assertive, question and answer enter into a tautological
balance: the divine sign finds itself completely absorbed in
its hearing. Then the mantic act concludes, for, returning the
deficiency from sign to sign, it has succeeded in including
within its system this empty and yet significant place called
the zero degree of the sign: restored to signification, the divine
vacuum can no longer threaten, alter, or decentralize the
plenitude which is part of every closed language.

[11] Ignatius's code of tears: a = tears before mass (*antes*); l =
tears during mass; d = tears after mass (*despues*); l— = meager tears,
etc.

FOURIER

Beginnings

I.   O NE DAY I was invited to eat a couscous with rancid butter; the rancid butter was customary; in certain regions it is an integral part of the couscous code. However, be it prejudice, or unfamiliarity, or digestive intolerance, I don't like rancidity. What to do? Eat it, of course, so as not to offend my host, but gingerly, in order not to offend the conscience of my disgust (since for disgust *per se* one needs some stoicism). In this difficult meal, Fourier would have helped me. On the one hand, intellectually, he would have persuaded me of three things: the first is that the rancidness of couscous is in no way an idle, futile, or trivial question, and that debating it is no more futile than debating Transubstantiation;[1] the second is that by forcing me to lie about my likes (or dislikes), society is manifesting its *falseness,* i.e., not only its hypocrisy (which is banal) but also the vice of the social mechanism whose gearing is faulty; the third, that this same society cannot rest until it has guaranteed (how? Fourier has clearly explained it, but it must be admitted that it hasn't worked) the exercise of my manias, whether "bizarre" or "minor," like those of people who like old chickens, the eater of horrid things (like the astronomer Lalande, who liked to

[1] "First we will deal with the puerility of these battles over the superiority of sweet cream or little pies; we might reply that the debate will be no more ridiculous than our Religious Wars over Transubstantiation" (VII, 346).

eat live spiders), the fanatics about butter, pears, bergamots, Ankles, or "Baby Dolls."[2] On the other hand, practically, Fourier would at once have put an end to my embarrassment (being torn between my good manners and my lack of taste for rancid things) by taking me from my meal (where, in addition, I was stuck for hours, a barely tolerable situation against which Fourier protested) and sending me to the Anti-Rancid group, where I would be allowed to eat fresh couscous as I liked without bothering anyone—which would not have kept me from preserving the best of relations with the Rancid group, whom I would henceforth consider as not at all "ethnic," foreign, strange, at for example a great couscous tournament, at which couscous would be the "theme," and where a jury of gastrosophers would decide on the superiority of rancid over fresh (I almost said: *normal,* but for Fourier, and this is his victory, there is no normality).[3]

[2] "Ankles" are men who like to scratch their mistress's ankle (VII, 335); the "Baby Doll" is a sixty-year-old man who, desirous of being treated like a spoiled child, wants the soubrette to punish him by "gently patting his patriarchal buttocks" (VII, 334).

[3] Fourier would, I am sure, have been enraptured at my friend Abd el Kebir's entry into the couscous tournament, in defense of the Rancid side, in a letter I received from him:

"I am not a Rancist either. I prefer couscous with pumpkin, and a light sprinkling of raisins—well blended, of course—and that produces: an insubordination of the expression.

"The apparent instability of the Moroccan peasant's culinary system proceeds, dear friend, from the fact that rancid butter is made in a strange underground hearth at the intersection of cosmic time and the time of consumption. Rancid butter is a kind of decomposed property, pleasing to interior monologue.

"Dug out in handfuls, rancid butter is worked in the following circular rite: a huge and magnificent ball of couscous is ejaculated into the throat to such an extent that the rancidity is neutralized. Fourier would call it a double-focus ellipse.

"This is why the peasant works to get rid of it: the parabole means a surplus, since the earth belongs to God. He inters the fresh butter, then extracts it when the time is ripe. However, the female is the one, the squatter, always squatting down, who carries out the operation

II.   Fourier likes compotes, fine weather, perfect melons, the little spiced pastries known as *mirlitons,* and the company of lesbians. Society and nature hinder these tastes a bit: sugar is (or was) expensive (more expensive than bread), the French climate is insupportable except in May, September, and October, we know no sure method of detecting a melon's quality, in Civilization little pastries bring on indigestion, lesbians are proscribed and, blind for a long time as far as he himself was concerned, Fourier did not know until very late in life that he liked them. Thus the world must be remade for my pleasure: my pleasure will be simultaneously the ends and the means: in organizing it, in distributing it, I shall overwhelm it.

III.   Everywhere we travel, on every occasion on which we feel a desire, a longing, a lassitude, a vexation, it is possible to ask Fourier, to wonder: What would he have said about it? What would he make of this place, this adventure? Here am I one evening in a southern Moroccan hotel: some hundred meters outside the populous, tattered, dusty town, a park filled with rare scents, a blue pool, flowers, quiet bungalows, hordes of discreet servants. In Harmony, what would that give? First of all, this: there would come to this place all who have this strange liking, this low mania for dim lights in the woods, candle-lit dinners, a staff of native servants, night frogs, and a camel in a meadow beneath the window.

---

from above. Slow and painstaking preparation, making my couscous taste rather androgynous.

"Thus, I agree to act within its limits: the rancid is an imperative fantasy. The pleasure is in eating with the group.

"Relating this manner of conserving butter underground to a traditional practice of mental healing, the frenzied madman is buried for a day or two, left almost naked, without food. When he is brought out, he is often reborn or really dies. Between heaven and earth there are signs to be seen for those who know.

"The high price put on couscous—a truly enigmatic material—obliges me to sign off and to send you my friendly wishes."

Then this rectification: the Harmonians would scarcely have need of this place, luxurious owing to its temperature (spring in mid-winter), because, by acting on the atmosphere, by modifying the polar cap, this exotic climate could be transported to Jouy-en-Josas or Gif-sur-Yvette. Finally, this compromise: at certain times during the year, hordes of people, driven by a taste for travel and adventure, would descend upon the idyllic motel and there hold their councils of love and gastronomy (it would be just the place for our couscous investigations). From which, once again, it emerges: that Fourierist pleasure is the end of the tablecloth: pull the slightest futile incident, provided it concerns your happiness, and all the rest of the world will follow: its organization, its limits, its values; this sequence, this fatal induction which ties the most tenuous inflection of our desire to the broadest sociality, this unique space in which fantasy and the social combinative are trapped, this is very precisely *systematics* (but not, as we shall see, the system); with Fourier, impossible to relax without constructing a theory about it. And this: in Fourier's day none of the Fourierist system had been achieved, but today? Caravans, crowds, the collective search for fine climate, pleasure trips, exist: in a derisory and rather atrocious form, the organized tour, the planting of a vacation club (with its classed population, its planned pleasures) is there in some fairy-tale site; in the Fourierist utopia there is a twofold reality, realized as a farce by mass society: *tourism* —the just ransom of a fantasmatic system which has "forgotten" politics, whereas politics pays it back by "forgetting" no less systematically to "calculate" for our pleasure. It is in the grip of these two forgettings, whose confrontation determines total futility, insupportable emptiness, that we are still floundering.

The Calculation of Pleasure

The motive behind all Fourierist construction (all combination) is not justice, equality, liberty, etc., it is pleasure.

Fourierism is not a radical eudaemonism. Fourierist pleasure (*positive happiness*) is very easy to define: it is sensual pleassure: "amorous freedom, good food, insouciance, and the other delights that the Civilized do not even dream of coveting because philosophy has taught them to treat the desire for true pleasures as vice."[4] Fourierist sensuality is, above all, oral. Of course, the two major sources of pleasure are equally Love and Food, always in tandem; however, although Fourier pushes the claims of erotic freedom, he does not describe it sensually; whereas food is lovingly fantasized in detail (compotes, *mirlitons,* melons, pears, lemonades); and Fourier's speech itself is sensual, it progresses in effusiveness, enthusiasm, throngs of words, verbal gourmandise (neologism is an erotic act, which is why he never fails to arouse the censure of pedants).

This Fourierist pleasure is commodious, *it stands out:* easily isolated from the heteroclite hotchpotch of causes, effects, values, protocols, habits, alibis, it appears throughout in its sovereign purity: mania (the ankle scratcher, the filth eater, the "Baby Doll") is never captured save through the pleasure it procures for its partners, and this pleasure is never encumbered with other images (absurdities, inconveniences, difficulties); in short, there is no metonymy attached to it: pleasure is what it is, nothing more. The emblematic ceremony of this isolation of essence would be a *museum orgy:* it consists of a simple exposition of the desirable, "a séance

[4] Let us briefly recall that in the Fourierist lexicon, *Civilization* has a precise (numbered) meaning: the word designates the 5th period of the 1st phase (Infancy of Mankind), which comes between the period of the federal patriarchate (the birth of large agriculture and manufacturing industry) and that of guaranteeism or demi-association (industry by association). Whence a broader meaning: in Fourier, *Civilization* is synonymous with wretched barbarism and designates the state of his own day (and ours); it contrasts with universal Harmony (2nd and 3rd phases of mankind). Fourier believed himself to be at the axis of Barbaric Civilization and Harmony.

wherein notable lovers lay bare the most remarkable thing they have. A woman whose only beautiful feature is her bosom exposes only the bosom and is covered elsewhere . . ." (we refrain from commenting on the fetishist character of this framework, evident enough; his intention not analytical but merely ethical, Fourier would not deign to take fetishism into a symbolic, reductive system: that would be merely a mania *along with* others, and not inferior or superior to them).

Fourierist pleasure is free from evil: it does not include vexation, in the Sadian manner, but on the contrary dissipates it; his discourse is one of "general well-being": for example, in the war of love (game and theater), out of delicacy, in order not to disturb, no flags or leaders are captured. If, however, in Harmony, one chances to suffer, the entire society will attempt to divert you: have you had some failure in love, have you been turned down, the Bacchantes, Adventuresses, and other pleasure corporations will surround you and lead you off, instantly efface the harm that has befallen you (they exercise, Fourier says, philanthropy). But if someone has a mania to harass? Should they be allowed? The pleasure of harassing is due to a congestion; Harmony will decongest the passions, sadism will be reabsorbed: Dame Strogonoff had the unpleasant habit of harassing her beautiful slave by piercing her breast with pins; in fact, it was counter-passion: Dame Strogonoff was in love with her victim without knowing it: Harmony, by authorizing and favoring Sapphic loves, would have relieved her of her sadism. Yet a final threat: satiety: how to *sustain* pleasure? "How act so as to have a continually renewed appetite? Here lies the secret of Harmonian politics." This secret is twofold: on the one hand, change the race and, through the over-all benefits of the societal diet (based on meats and fruits, with very little bread), form physiologically stronger men, fit for the renewal of pleasures, capable of digesting more quickly, of being hungry more frequently; and on the other hand, vary pleasures incessantly (never more than two hours at the same task), and from all these successive pleasures make one sole continual pleasure.

Here we have pleasure alone and triumphant, it reigns over all. Pleasure cannot be measured, it is not subject to quantification, its nature is the *overmuch* ("Our fault is not, as has been believed, to desire *overmuch,* but to desire *too little* . . ."); it is itself the measurement: "feeling" depends on pleasure: "The privation of the sensual need degrades feeling," and "full satisfaction in material things is the only way to elevate the feelings": counter-Freudianism: "feeling" is not the sublimating transformation of a lack, but on the contrary the panic effusion of an acme of satiety. Pleasure overcomes Death (pleasures will be sensual in the afterlife), it is the Federator, what operates the solidarity of the living and the dead (the happiness of the defunct will begin only with that of the living, they having in a way to *await* the others: no happy dead so long as on earth the living are not happy; a view of a generosity, a "charity" that no religious eschatology has dared). Pleasure is, lastly, the everlasting principle of social organization: whether, negatively, it induces a condemnation of all society, however progressive, that neglects it (such as Owen's experiment at New Lamarck, denounced as "too severe" because the societaries went barefoot), whether, positively, pleasures are made *affairs of State* (*pleasures* and not *leisure:* this is what separates—fortunately—the Fourierist Harmony from the modern State, where the pious organization of leisure time corresponds to a relentless censure of pleasure); pleasure results, in fact, from a *calculation,* an operation that for Fourier is the highest form of social organization and mastery; this calculation is the same as that of all societal theory, whose practice is to transform work into pleasure (and not to suspend work for the sake of leisure time): the barrier that separates work from pleasure in Civilization crumbles, there is a paradigmatic fall, philosophical conversion of the unpleasant into the attractive (taxes will be paid "as readily as the busy mother sees to those foul but attractive duties her infant demands"), and pleasure itself becomes an exchange value, since Harmony recognizes and honors, by the name of *Angelicate,* collective prostitution: it is in a way the monad of energy which in its thrust and scope ensures the advance of society.

Since pleasure is the Unique, to reveal pleasure is itself a unique duty: Fourier stands alone against everyone (especially against all the Philosophers, against all Libraries), he alone is right, and being right is the desirable thing: "Is it not to be desired that I alone am right, against everyone?" From the Unique derives the incendiary character of pleasure: it burns, shocks, frightens to speak of it: how many are the statements about the mortal shock brought on by the over-abrupt revelation of pleasure! What precautions, what preparations of writing! Fourier experiences a kind of prophylactic obligation for dispassion (poorly observed, by the way: he imagines his "calculations" are boring and that reassures him, whereas they are delightful); whence an incessant restraint of the discourse: "fearing to allow you to glimpse the vastness of these pleasures, I have only dissertated on . . ." etc.: Fourier's discourse is never just propaedeutic, so blazing with splendor is its object, its center:[5] articulated on pleasure, the sectarian world is *dazzling.*

The area of Need is *Politics,* the area of Desire is what Fourier calls *Domestics.* Fourier has chosen Domestics over Politics, he has constructed a domestic utopia (but can a

[5] "If we could suddenly see this arranged Order, this work of God as it will be seen in its full functioning . . . it is not to be doubted that many of the Civilized would be struck dead by the violence of their ecstasy. The description [of the 8th Society] alone could inspire in many of them, the women in particular, an enthusiasm that would approach frenzy; it could render them indifferent to amusements, unsuited to the labors of Civilization" (I, 65).

utopia be otherwise? can a utopia ever be political? isn't politics: *every language less one,* that of Desire? In May 1968, there was a proposal to one of the groups that were spontaneously formed at the Sorbonne to study *Domestic Utopia*— they were obviously thinking of Fourier; to which the reply was made that the expression was too "studied," *ergo* "bourgeois"; politics is what forecloses desire, save to achieve it in the form of neurosis: political neurosis or, more exactly: the neurosis of politicizing).

Money Creates Happiness

In Harmony, not only is wealth redeemed, but it is also magnified, it participates in a play of felicitous metaphors, lending the Fourierist demonstrations either the ceremonial brio of jewels ("the diamond star in a radiant triangle," the decoration of amatory sainthood, i.e., widespread prostitution) or the modesty of the sou ("20 sous to Racine for his tragedy *Phèdre*": multiplied, true, by all the cantons that have chosen to honor the poet); the operations connected with money are themselves motifs in a delectable game: in the game of love, that of the redemption (repurchase) of captives. Money participates in the brilliance of pleasure ("The senses cannot have their full indirect scope without the intervention of money"): money is desirable, as in the best days of civilized corruption, beyond which it perpetuates itself by virtue of a splendid and "incorruptible" fantasy.

Curiously detached from commerce, from exchange, from the economy, Fourierist money is an analogic (poetic) metal, the sum of happiness. Its exaltation is obviously a countermeasure: it is because all (civilized) Philosophy has condemned money that Fourier, destroyer of Philosophy and critic of Civilization, rehabilitates it: *the love of wealth* being a pejorative *topos* (at the price of a constant hypocrisy: Seneca, the man who possessed 80 million sesterces, declared that one must instantly rid oneself of wealth), Fourier turns contempt into praise:[6] marriage, for example, is a ridiculous ceremony,[7] save "when a man marries a very rich woman; then there is occasion for rejoicing"; everything, where money is concerned, seems to be conceived in view of this counter-discourse, frankly scandalous in relation to the literary constraints of the admonition: "Search out the tangible wealth, gold, silver, precious metals, jewels, and objects of luxury despised by philosophers."[8]

However, this fact of discourse is not rhetorical: it has that energy of language that in writing makes the discourse waver, it forms the basis for the major transgression against which *everyone*—Christians, Marxists, Freudians—for whom money continues to be an accursed matter, fetish, excrement, has spoken out: who would dare defend money? There is *no discourse* with which money can be compatible. Because it is completely solitary (Fourier does not find on this point among his colleagues, "literary agitators," any co-maniac), Fourierist transgression lays bare the most secret area of the Civilized conscience. Fourier exalted money because for him the image of happiness was properly furnished with the mode of life of the wealthy: a shocking view today, in the eyes of the contestants themselves, who condemn all pleasure induced from the bourgeois model. We know that metonymy (contagion)

[6] "Whence a conclusion that may seem facetious but that will nonetheless be rigorously demonstrated; in the 18 societies of Combined Order, the most basic quality for the triumph of truth is the love of wealth" (I, 70). "Glory and science are truly desirable, of course, but quite insufficient when unaccompanied by fortune. Fame, trophies, and other illusions do not lead to happiness, which consists first of all in the possession of wealth . . ." (I, 14).

[7] "One must be born in Civilization to tolerate the sight of those indecent customs known as marriages, where one sees the simultaneous coincidence of magistrate and priest with the fools and drunks of the neighborhood" (I, 174).

[8] Since the coming of Harmony was imminent, Fourier counseled the Civilized to profit at once from the few goods of Civilization; this is the age-old theme (reversed, i.e., positive): Live to the full now, tomorrow is another day, it is futile to save, to keep, to transmit.

is the purview of Error (of religion); Fourier's radical materialism stems from his constant, vigilant refusal of any metonymy. For him, money is not a conductor of sickness but merely the dry, pure element in a combinative to be reordered.

Inventor, Not Writer

To remake the world (including Nature), Fourier mobilized: an intolerance (for Civilization), a form (classification), a standard (pleasure), an imagination (the "scene"), a discourse (his book). All of which pretty well defines the action of the signifier—or the signifier in action. This action continually makes visible on the page a glaring lack, that of science and politics, that is, of the signified.[9] What Fourier lacks (for that matter voluntarily) points in return to what we ourselves lack when we reject Fourier: to be ironic about Fourier is always—even from the scientific point of view— to censure the signifier. Political and Domestic (the name of Fourier's system),[10] science and utopia, Marxism and Fourierism, are like two nets whose meshes are of different sizes. On the one hand, Fourier allows to pass through all the science that Marx collects and develops; from the political point of view (and above all since Marxism has given an indelible name to its shortcomings), Fourier is completely *off to one side,* unrealistic and immoral. However, the other, facing, net allows pleasure, which Fourier collects, to pass through.[11] Desire and Need pass through, as though the two

[9] ". . . seek the good only in operations having no relationship with the administration or with the priesthood, that rest solely on industrial or domestic measures and that are compatible with any government, without having need of their intervention" (I, 5).

[10] ". . . to demonstrate the extreme facility of exiting from the civilized labyrinth, without political upheaval, without scientific effort, but by a purely domestic operation" (I, 126).

[11] ". . . sophists deceive us about their incompetency in calculations of amatory or petty politics, and occupy us exclusively with ambitious or major politics . . ." (IV, 51).

nets were alternatively superimposed, playing at topping hands. However, the relationship of Desire and Need is not *complementary* (were they fitted one into the other, everything would be perfect), but *supplementary:* each is the *excess* of the other. The *excess:* what does not pass through. For example, seen from today (i.e., *after* Marx), politics is a necessary purge; Fourier is the child who avoids the purge, who vomits it up.

The vomiting of politics is what Fourier calls Invention. Fourierist invention ("For me, I am an inventor, and not an orator") addresses the absolutely new, that about which nothing has yet been said. The rule of invention is a rule of refusal: to doubt absolutely (more than did Descartes, who, Fourier thought, never made more than a partial and misplaced use of doubt), to be in opposition with everything being done, to treat only of what has not been treated, to stand apart from "literary agitators," Book People, to preach what Opinion holds to be *impossible.* It is in sum for this purely structural reason (*old/new*) and through a simple constraint of the discourse (to speak only where there has not yet been speech) that Fourier is silent about politics. Fourierist invention is a fact of writing, a deploying of the signifier. These words should be understood in the modern sense: Fourier repudiates *the writer,* i.e., the certified manager of good writing, of literature, he who guarantees decorative union and thus the fundamental separation of substance and form; in calling himself an inventor ("I am not a writer, but an inventor"), he places himself at the limit of meaning, what we today call Text. Perhaps, following Fourier, we should henceforth call *inventor* (and not *writer* or *philosopher*) he who proposes new formulae and thereby invests, by fragments, *immensely and in detail,* the space of the signifier.

The Meta-Book

The meta-book is the book that talks about the book. Fourier spends his time talking about his book in such a way

that the work of Fourier that we read, indissolubly blending
the two discourses, finally forms an autonomous book, in
which form incessantly states form.

Fourier escorts his book a long way. For example, he
imagines a dialogue between bookseller and client. Or elsewhere, knowing his book will be brought into court, he establishes a whole institutional system of defense (judge, jury,
lawyers) and diffusion (the rich reader who wants to clear
up some doubts for himself will call in the author to give
lessons, as in sciences and the arts: "a kind of relationship
without consequences, as with a merchant from whom one
buys": after all, it is something like what a writer does today,
going off on lecture tours to repeat words he has stated in
writing).

As for the book itself, he posits rhetoric, i.e., the adapta-
tion of types of discourse to types of readers: the *exposition*
is addressed to the "Curious" (that is, to studious men); the
descriptions (insights into the delights of private Destinies)
are addressed to Voluptuaries or Sybarites; the *confirmation,*
pointing up the blunders of the Civilized in thrall to the Spirit
of Commerce, is addressed to the Critics. We can distinguish
bits of *perspective* and bits of *theory* (I, 160); there will be
insights (abstract), *summaries* (half concrete), *elaborate
dissertations* (bodies of doctrine). It follows that the book
(a somewhat Mallarméan view) is not only pieced out, articulated (a banal structure), but, further, mobile, subject to
a rule of *intermittent* actualization: the chapters will be inverted, the reading will be speeded up (expedited movement)
or slowed down, according to the class of readers we want to
reach; at its limit, the book is composed of nothing but jumps,
full of holes like Fourier's manuscripts (especially *Le
Nouveau Monde amoureux*), whose words are constantly
missing, eaten by mice, and which therefore have the dimensions of an infinite cryptogram whose key will be given later.

This reminds us of reading in the Middle Ages, based on
the work's legal discontinuity: not only was the ancient text

(subject of medieval reading) *broken up* and its fragments then capable of being diversely combined, but, further, it was normal to conduct on any subject two independent and concurrent discourses, shamelessly put in a redundant relationship: Donatus's *ars minor* (abridged) and *ars major* (extended), the Modistes' *modi minores* and *modi majores;* this is the Fourierist opposition of insight-abridgment and dissertation. Yet the effect of this doubling up is twisted, paradoxical. We would expect that like any redundancy it would completely cover the subject, fill it out and end it (what can be added to a discourse that essentializes its purpose in résumé form and develops it in the form of an elaborate dissertation?). Now the contrary: the duplicity of the discourse produces an *interstice* through which the subject leaks away: Fourier spends his time in withholding the decisive utterance of his doctrine, concerning it he gives us only examples, seductions, "appetizers"; the message of his book is the announcement of a forthcoming message: *wait a little longer, I will tell you the essential very soon.* This method of writing could be called *counter-paralypse* (the paralypse is the rhetorical figure that consists in stating what one is not going to say and thus stating what one pretends not to say: *I shall not speak of* . . . followed by three pages). The paralypse implies the conviction that the indirect is a profitable mode of language; however, Fourier's countermarch, other than that it obviously translates the neurotic fear of failure (like that of a man afraid to jump—which Fourier, transferring to the reader, utters as the mortal fear of pleasure), points out the vacuum of language: caught in the toils of the meta-book, his book is *without subject:* its signified is dilatory, incessantly withdrawn further away: only the signifier remains, stretching out of sight, *in the book's future.*

The Old Shoe Ablaze

Somewhere, Fourier speaks of "nocturnal furnishings." What do I care that this expression is the trace of an earthshaking transport? I am carried away, dazzled, convinced by a kind of *charm* in the expression, which is its delight. Fourier is crammed full of these delights: no discourse was ever *happier*. With Fourier, the expression derives its felicity (and ours) from a kind of upheaval: it is excentric, displaced, it lives on its own, outside its context (the context, the semanticists' puzzler, has all the ingratitude of law: it reduces polysemy, clips the wings of the signifier: doesn't all poetry consist in liberating the word from its context? doesn't all philosophy consist in putting it back?). I do not resist these pleasures, they seem "true" to me: I have been "taken in" by the form.

Of what do these charms consist: of a counter-rhetoric, that is, a way of contriving figures by introducing into their code a "grain" (of sand, of madness). Let us here, once again (after many centuries of rhetorical classification), distinguish tropes (or simple metaboles) and figures (or ornaments that act upon an entire syntagm). Fourier's metaphorical vein is the path of truth; it supplies him with simple metaphors of a definitive precision ("from delivery vans we derive *fatigue dress,* the gray cloak and trousers"), it clarifies meaning (monological function), but at the same time and contradictorily it clarifies *ad infinitum* (poetical function), not only because the metaphor is drawn out, orchestrated ("Nocturnal furnishings will be considerably assorted and composed of our vivid and variously colored moons, next to which Phoebe will appear as what she is, a pale ghost, a sepulchral lamp, a Swiss cheese. One would have to have as bad taste as the Civilized do to admire this pallid mummy"), but further and above all because the Fourierist syntagm simultaneously produces a sonorous pleasure and a logical vertigo. Fourier's enumerations (for his verbal "delirium," based on calculation, is basically enumerative) always contain a preposterous point, a twist, a wrinkle: ". . . the ostrich, the deer, the jerboa . . .": why the jerboa, unless for the sonorous flourish at the end, for the sound? "And what can Hell in its fury in-

vent worse than the rattlesnake, the bug, the legion of insects
and reptiles, the sea monsters, poisons, plague, rabies, leprosy,
venereal disease, gout, and all the morbiferous virulences?":
the bug and the sea monster? Rattlesnakes and venereal
disease? This string of nonsense derives a final savor from the
morbiferous, plump and brilliant, more alimentary than fune-
real, both sensual and ridiculous (Molièresque), that crowns
it; for the enumerative *cumulus,* in Fourier, is as abrupt as the
movement of the head of an animal, a bird, a child who has
heard "something else": "There will remain only the useful
strains, like the whiting, the herring, the mackerel, sole, tuna,
tortoise, in short, all those that do not attack swimmers . . .":
what charms us is not the content (after all, there is no question that these fish are beneficent), but a certain turn that
makes the affirmation vibrate toward its opposite region: mis-
chievously, through an irresistible metonymy seizing the
words, a vague image becomes detached which, across the
denegation, reveals the whiting and the mackerel in the process of attacking a swimmer . . . (a properly surrealist
mechanism). Paradoxical, for it is always in the name of the
"concrete" that Civilization claims to teach the "mad," it is
always through the "concrete" that Fourier becomes absurd
and charming at once: the "concrete" is constructed in a
scene, the substance calls upon the practices metonymically
attached to it; the coffee break refers to the whole of civilized
bureaucracy: "Isn't it shocking to see thirty-year-old ath-
letes crouched over desks and transporting a cup of coffee with
their hairy arms, as though there weren't women and children
to attend to the finicky functioning of offices and house-
holds?" This vivid representation provokes laughter because
it is out of proportion with its signified; hypotypose usually
serves to illustrate intense and noble passions (Racine:
"Imagine, Céphise . . ."); in Fourier, it is demonstrative; a
kind of anacoluthon intervenes between the domestic detail
of the example and the scope of the utopian plan. This is the

secret of these amusing syntagms frequent in Fourier (in Sade
too) that join in a single sentence a very ambitious thought
and a very futile object; starting from the notion of the culinary contests in Harmony ("thesis meals"), Fourier continues to concoct strange and delicious, ridiculous and decisive syntagms, in which the tiny pastries (which he so liked,
mirlitons) are associated with highly abstract terms ("the 44
systems of tiny pastries," "the batches of tiny pastries anath-
emized by the council," "the tiny pastries adopted by the
Council of Babylon," etc.). Very precisely, this is what we
can now call *paragrammatics:* namely, the superimpression
(in dual hearing) of two languages that are ordinarily foreclosed to each other, the braid formed by two classes of
words whose traditional hierarchy is not annulled, balanced,
but—what is more subversive—disoriented: Council and
System lend their nobility to tiny pastries; tiny pastries lend
their futility to Anathema, a sudden contagion *deranges* the
institution of language.

The transgression Fourier commits goes even further. The
frivolous object he promotes to demonstrative rank is very
often a *base* object. This conversion is justified because Harmony recuperates what Civilization disdains and transforms
it into a delightful good ("If the Vaucluse phalanstery har-
vests 50,000 melons or watermelons, almost 10,000 of them
will be set aside for its own consumption, 30,000 for exporta-
tion, and 10,000 will be of inferior grade and divided among
horses, cats, and for fertilizer": here we find that art of enumerative cadence we have just mentioned: Fourierist enumeration is always reverse conundrum: what is the difference between a horse, a cat, and fertilizer? None, for the function of
all three is to reabsorb inferior-grade melons). Thus a poetics
of rubbish is constructed, magnified by the societary economy
(e.g., the old marinated chickens). Fourier knows this poetics
well: he knows the emblems of rubbish, the old shoe, the rag,
the sewer: an entire episode in *Le Nouveau Monde amoureux*

(VII, 362 *et seq.*) hymns the exploits of the new crusaders, dealers in old shoes and boot cleaners, whose arrival at the Euphrates crossing is greeted by a magnificent display of fireworks "ending with an old shoe ablaze, beneath which is the legend: Long live pious cobblers."

Naturally, Fourier was aware of the "ridiculousness" of his demonstrative objects (of his rhetoric);[12] he was well aware that the bourgeoisie is devoted to the hierarchical division of languages, objects, and usages as strongly as it is to those of class, that nothing is worse in their eyes than the crime of lèse-language, and that one has only to join a noble (abstract) word and a base (denoting a sensual or repulsive object) term to be sure of loosing their zeal as proprietors (of "fine" language); he knew that people made fun of his faithful melons, of the triumph of his leathery fowl, of the English debt paid off in hens' eggs. Yet he assumed the incongruity of his demonstrations with a certain martyred air (the martyrdom of the inventor). Thus to the paragrammaticism of his examples (interweaving two exclusive languages, one noble, one outcast), must be added a final, infinitely dizzier, ambiguity: that of their utterance. Where is Fourier? in the invention of the example (old marinated chickens)? in the indignation he feels at the laughter of others? In our reading, which simultaneously encompasses the ridicule and his defense? The loss of the subject in the writing has never been more complete (the subject becoming totally irreparable) than in these utterances where the disconnection of the utter-

---

12 "This respectable convoy of cobblers marches after them in pomp and the finest boat is loaded with their baggage and this is the arm upon which they lean to win the palms of true glory. Bah! glory in old shoes, our Civilized will say; I was expecting this stupid response. And what fruit have they gleaned from the trophies of St. Louis and Bonaparte who have led immense armies vast distances only to have them drown in their trophies after having ravaged the country and been execrated by it?" (VII, 364).

ance occurs *ad infinitum,* without a brake, on the model of
the game of topping hands or the game of "rock, scissors,
paper": texts whose "ridiculousness" or "stupidity" is based
on no certain utterance and over which, consequently, the
reader can never gain any advantage (Fourier, Flaubert).
"God," Fourier says, "displays a subtle and judicious irony
in creating certain products that are enigmatic in quality, like
the melon, made for the innocent mystification of banquets
ill suited to divine methods, without in any way deceiving the
gastronomes who cleave to the divine or societary diet" [al-
lusion to the difficulty that exists in choosing a good melon,
"such a perfidious fruit for the Civilized"]. "I do not mean
to say that God created the melon solely for the sake of this
jest, but it is part of that fruit's many uses. Irony is never
overlooked in the calculations of nature. . . . The melon has
among its properties that of *ironic harmony* . . ." (in short,
the melon is an element of a *writing*). What reader can hope
to *dominate* such an utterance—adopt it as a laughable or a
critical object, *dictate to it,* in a word?—in the name of *what
other language?*

Hieroglyphics

Fourier wants to decipher the world in order to remake it
(for how remake it without deciphering it?).

Fourierist deciphering starts from the most difficult of situations, which is not so much the latency of signs as their content. There is a saying of Voltaire that Fourier refers to in
this regard: "But what obscure night still enveileth nature?";
now, in this veil finally there is less the notion of mask than
of a cloth. Once again, the task of the logothete, of the
founder of language, is an endless cutting up of the text: the
primary operation is to "grab" the cloth in order then to
pull on it (to pull it off).

We must therefore in some measure make a distinction between deciphering and cutting up. Deciphering refers to a

pregnant depth, to an area of relationships, to a distribution. In Fourier, deciphering is postulated, but in a completely minor way: it concerns the lies and pretenses of the Civilized classes: thus the "secret principles" of the bourgeois "who begins by debiting a hundred lies in his shop by virtue of the principles of free trade. Hence a bourgeois goes to hear Mass and returns to debit three to four hundred lies, to trick and steal from thirty or so buyers in line with the secret principle of businessmen: we are not working for glory, we want money" (VII, 246). Quite another thing, and of quite another order of importance, is cutting up—or systematization (putting to a system); this reading, an essential part of the Fourierist task, concerns all of Nature (societies, sentiments, forms, natural kingdoms) as it represents the total space of Harmony—Fourier's man being totally incorporated into the universe, including the stars; this is no longer a denunciatory, reductive reading (limited to the moral falsehoods of the bourgeoisie), but an exalting, integrating, restorative reading, extended to the plethora of universal forms.

Is the "real" the object of this second reading? We are accustomed to considering the "real" and the residue as identical: the "unreal," the fantasmatic, the ideological, the verbal, the proliferating, in short, the "marvelous," may conceal from us the "real," rational, infrastructural, schematic; from real to unreal there may be the (self-seeking) production of a screen of arabesques, whereas from unreal to real there may be critical reduction, an alethic, scientific movement, as though the real were at once more meager and more essential than the superstructures with which we have covered it. Obviously, Fourier is working on a conceptual material whose constitution denies this contrast and which is that of the *marvelous real*. This marvelous real is contrasted with the marvelous ideal of novels; it corresponds to what we might call, contrasting it directly with the novel, the novelesque. This marvelous real very precisely is the signifier, or if one prefers, "reality," characterized, relative to the scientific real, by its fantasmatic train. Now, the category under which this novelesque begins to be read is the *hieroglyphic,* different from the symbol as the signifier can be from the full, mystified sign.

The hieroglyph (the theory of which is set forth principally in the *Théorie des Quatre Mouvements,* I, 31 *et seq.* and 286 *et seq.*) postulates a formal and arbitrary correspondence (it depends on Fourier's free will: it is an idiolectal concept) between the various realms of the universe, for example between forms (circle, ellipse, parabola, hyperbola), colors, musical notes, passions (friendship, love, parental, ambition), the races of animals, the stars, and the periods of societal phylogenesis. The arbitrary obviously resides in the attribution: why is the ellipse the geometric hieroglyph for love? the parabola for parenthood? Yet this arbitrary is just as relative as is that of linguistic signs: we believe there to be an arbitrary correspondence between the signifier/pear tree/and the signified "pear tree," between some Melanesian tribe and its totem (bear, god), because we spontaneously (i.e., by virtue of historical, ideological determinations) imagine the world in substitute, paradigmatic, analogical terms, and not in serial, associative, homological—in short, poetic—terms. Fourier has this second imagination; for him, the basis of meaning is not substitution, equivalence, but the proportional series; just as the signifier /pear tree/ or the signifier *bear* is *relatively* motivated if taken in the series *pear tree–plum tree–apple tree* or in the series *bear–dog–tiger,* so Fourierist hieroglyphics, detached from any univocity, accede to language, i.e., to a system both conventional and reasonable. The hieroglyphic, in fact, implies a complete theory of meaning (whereas only too often, relying on the presence of the dictionary , we reduce meaning to a substitution): hieroglyphics, says Fourier, can be explained in three ways: (1) *by contrast* (beehive/wasp's nest, elephant/rhinoceros): this is the paradigm: the beehive is *marked* with productivity, a characteristic absent in the wasp's nest; the elephant is marked with lengthy defenses, a trait reduced to a short horn in the rhinoceros; (2) *by alliance* (the dog and the sheep, the pig and the truffle, the donkey and the thistle): this is the syntagm, metonymy: these elements usually go together; (3) lastly, *by progression* (branches: giraffe, stag, buck, roebuck, reindeer, etc.): this, foreign to linguistic classification, is the *series,* a kind of extended paradigm, consisting of differences and proximities, out of which Fourier creates the very principle of societal organization, which basically consists in putting in a phalanstery contrasting groups of individuals, each group linked by an affinity: for example, the sectine of Flowerlets, amateurs of small, varied flowers, contrasted to but coexisting with the Rosist sectine: it might be said that the series is an actualized, syntagmatized paradigm, by virtue of the number of its terms, not only *livable* (whereas the semantic paradigm is subject to the law of rival, inexpiable opposites, which cannot cohabit), but even *felicitous.* Progression (the series) is undoubtedly what Fourier adds to meaning (as linguists describe it for us), and conseqeuntly, what frustrates its arbitrary nature. Why, for example, in Association, is the giraffe the hieroglyph for Truth (I, 286)? A farfetched notion and assuredly unjustifiable if we try, desperately, to discover some affinitive or even contrasting trait shared by Truth and this huge mammiferous ungulant. The explanation is that the giraffe is caught up in a system of homologies: Association having the beaver as its practical hieroglyph (because of its associative and constructive abilities) and the peacock as its visual hieroglyph (because of the spread of its nuances), we need, across from but yet in the same series, that of animals, a properly unfunctional element, a kind of neuter, a zero degree of zoological symbolism: this is the giraffe, as useless as the Truth is in Civilization; whence a counter-giraffe (complex term of contrast): this is the Reindeer, from which we derive every imaginable service (in the societary order there will even be a new animal created, even more ecumenical than the Reindeer: the Anti-Giraffe).

So replaced in the history of the sign, the Fourierist construction posits the rights of a baroque semantics, i.e., open to the proliferation of the signifier, infinite and yet structured.

Liberal?

The combination of differences implies the respecting of the individuation of each term: there is no attempt to redress, to correct, to annul taste, whatever it may be (however "bizarre" it may be); quite the contrary, it is affirmed, it is emphasized, it is recognized, it is legalized, it is reinforced by associating everyone who wishes to indulge it: taste being thus incorporated, it is allowed to act in opposition to other tastes at once affinitive and different: a competitive game (of intrigue, but *coded*) is initiated between the amateurs of bergamot pears and the amateurs of butter pears: to the satisfaction of a simple taste (a liking for pears) is then added the exercise of other, formal, combinative passions: for example, *cabalistics,* or the passion for intrigues, and *butterfly,* if there are unstable Harmonians who take pleasure in switching from the bergamot pear to the butter pear.

From this semantic construction of the world it follows that, in Fourier's eyes, "association" is not a "humanist" principle: it is not a matter of bringing together everyone with the same mania ("co-maniacs") so that they can be comfortable together and can enchant each other by narcissistically gazing at one another; on the contrary, it is a matter of associating to combine, to contrast. The Fourierist coexistence of passions is not based on a liberal principle. There is no noble demand to "understand," to "admit" the passions of others (or to ignore them, indeed). The goal of Harmony is neither to further the conflict (by associating through similitude), nor to reduce it (by sublimating, sweetening, or normalizing the passions), nor yet to transcend it (by "understanding" the other person), but to exploit it for the greatest pleasure of all and without hindrance to anyone. How? By playing at it: by making a text of the conflictual.

Passions

Passion (character, taste, mania) is the irreducible unity of the Fourierist combinative, the absolute grapheme of the utopian text. Passion is *natural* (nothing to be corrected about it, unless to produce a *contra-naturam,* which is what occurs in Civilization). Passion is *clean* (its being is pure, strong, shapely: only Civilized philosophy advises flaccid, apathetic passions, controls, and compromises). Passion is *happy* ("Happiness . . . consists in having many passions and ample means to satisfy them," I, 92).

Passion is not the idealized form of feeling, mania is not the monstrous form of passion. Mania (and even whim) is the very being of passion, the unit from which Attraction (attractive and attracting) is determined. Passion is neither deformable, nor transformable, nor reducible, nor measurable, nor substitutable: it is not a force, it is a number: there can be neither decomposition nor amalgamation of this happy, frank, natural monad, but only combination, up to the reunion of the *integral soul,* the trans-individual body of 1,620 characters.

The Tree of Happiness

The passions (810 for each sex) spring, like the branches of a tree (the classifier's fetish tree) from three main trunks: *lustful-ness,* which includes the passions of feeling (one for each of the five senses), *group-ness* (four basic passions: honor, friendship, love, and family), and *serial-ness* (three distributive passions). The entire combinative stems from these twelve passions (whose pre-eminence is not moral, merely structural).

The first nine passions are derived from classical psychology, but the latter, formal, three are a Fourierist invention. The Dissident (or Cabalistic) is a reflective enthusiasm, a passion for intrigue, a calculating mania, an art of exploiting differences, rivalries, conflicts (here there is no difficulty in recognizing the paranoid texture); it is the delight of courtesans, women, and philosophers (intellectuals), which is why it can also be called the Speculative. The Composite (actually less well defined than its fellows) is the passion for excess, for (sensual or sublime) exaltation, for multiplication; it can be called the Romantic. The Variating (or Alternating or Butterfly) is a need for periodic variety (changing occupation or pleasure every two hours); we might say that it is the disposition of the subject who does not devote himself to the "good object" in a stable manner: a passion whose mythical prototype is Don Juan: individuals who constantly change occupation, manias, affections, desires, "cruisers" who are incorrigible, unfaithful, renegade, subject to "moods," etc.: a passion disdained in Civilization, but one Fourier places very high: the one that permits ranging through many passions at once, and like an agile hand on a multiple keyboard, creating an *harmonious* (appropriately put) vibration throughout the integral soul; an agent of universal transition, it animates that type of happiness that is attributed to Parisian sybarites, *the art of living well and fast, the variety and interconnection of pleasures,* rapidity of movement (we recall that for Fourier the mode of life of the possessing class is the very model of happiness).

These three passions are formal: included in the classification, they ensure its functioning ("mechanics"), or more precisely still: its game. If we compare the aggregate of the passions to a deck of cards or a chess set (as did Fourier), the three distributive passions are in sum the rules of this game;

they state how to conciliate, balance, set in motion, and permit the transformation of the other passions, each of which would be nugatory in isolation, into a series of "brilliant and countless combinations." These rules of the game (these formal, distributive passions) are precisely the ones society rejects: they produce (the very sign of their excellence) "the characters accused of corruption, called libertines, profligates, etc.": as in Sade, it is syntax and syntax alone that produces the supreme immorality.

Thus the twelve radical passions (like the twelve notes in the scale). Naturally, there is a thirteenth (every good classifier knows he must have a supernumber in his chart and that he must make adjustments for the outcome of his system), which is the very trunk of the tree of passions: Unity-ness (or Harmonism). Unity-ness is the passion for unity, "the individual's tendency to reconcile his happiness with that of everything around him, and with every human type"; this supplementary passion produces the Originals, people who appear to be ill at ease in this world and who cannot accommodate themselves to the ways of Civilization; it is thus the passion of Fourier himself. Unity-ness is in no way a moral, recommendable passion (*love each other, unite with each other*), since the societal unit is a combinative, a structural game of differences; Unity-ness is in direct contrast to simplism, the vice of the Civilized spirit, "the use of the mind without the marvelous, or of the marvelous without the mind"; simplism "made Newton miss out on the discovery of the system of nature and Bonaparte on the conquest of the world." Simplism (or totalitarianism, or monologism) would today be either the censure of Need or the censure of Desire; which, in Harmony (in Utopia), would be answered by the combined science of one and the other.

Numbers

Fourier's authority, the Reference, the Citation, the Science, the Anterior Discourse that enables him to speak and to have personal authority concerning the "carelessness of 25 learned centuries that failed to conceive of it," is *calculation* (as for us today it is formalization). This calculation need not be extensive or complicated: it is a *petty calculation*. Why petty? Because although important (the happiness of mankind depends upon it), this calculation is simple. Further, pettiness includes the notion of a certain affectionate complacence: Fourier's petty calculation is the simple lever that opens up the fantasmagory of adorable detail.

Everything occurs as though Fourier were searching for the very notion of detail, as though he had found it in a numeration or frantic subdivision of every object that came into his mind, as though this object instantly released in him a number or a classification: it is like a conditioned reflex that comes into play apropos a whole crazy total: "In Rome in the time of Varro there were 278 contradictory opinions concerning true happiness." A question of illicit liaisons (in Civilization)? They exist for Fourier only if he enumerates them: "During the twelve years of bachelorhood, man forms on the average 12 liaisons of illicit love, around 6 of fornication and 6 adulterous, etc." Everything is a pretext for numbering, from the age of the world (80,000 years) to the number of characters in it (1,620).

The Fourierist number is not rounded off, and in fact this is what gives it its insanity (a minor sociological problem: why does our society consider a decimal number "normal" and an intradecimal number "irrational"? At what point does normality occur?). This insanity is often justified by the even more insane reasons Fourier gives in denying the arbitrary constants in his accounts, or, which is even crazier still, displaces this arbitrary by justifying not the number given, but the standard for it: the height of societary man will be 84 thumbs or 7 feet; why? we will never know, but the unit of measurement is pompously justified: "I am not being arbitrary in indicating the foot of the King of Paris as a natural measurement; it has this property because it is equal to the

32nd part of the water level in suction pumps" (here we find that sudden twisting of the syntagm, the anacoluthon, the audacious metonymy that makes Fourier's "charm": in the space of a few words, we have suction pumps mingled with the height of societary man). The number exalts, it is an operator of glory, as is the triangular number of the Trinity in the Jesuit mode, not because it enlarges (which would destroy the fascination with detail), but because it demultiplies: "Consequently, if we divide by 810 the number of 36 million which the population of France has attained, we will find that in this Empire there exist 45,000 individuals capable of equaling Homer, 45,000 capable of equaling Demosthenes, etc." Fourier is like a child (or an adult: the author of these lines, never having studied mathematics, has been very late in experiencing this feeling) discovering with enchantment the exorbitant power of combinatory analysis or geometrical progression. In the end, the number itself is not needed for this exaltation; one need only subdivide a class in order triumphantly to achieve this paradox: detail (literally: *minutia*) magnifies, like joy. It is a fury of expansion, of possession, and, in a word, of orgasm, by number, by classification: scarcely does an object appear than Fourier taxinomizes (we are tempted to say: sodomizes) it: is the husband unhappy in Civilized marriage? It is *immediately* for eight reasons (risk of unhappiness, expense, vigilance, monotony, sterility, widowhood, union, ignorance of his wife's infidelity). Does the word "harem" arise *currente calamo* into the sentence? *Immediately,* there are three classes of odalisks: honest women, petites bourgeoises, and courtesans. What happens to women over 18 years of age in Harmony? nothing, save to be *classified: Wives* (themselves subdivided into *constant, doubtful,* and *unfaithful*), *Misses* or *Demi-dames* (they change protectors, but successively, having only one at a time), and *Galantes* (both further subdivided); for both terms in the series, two taxinomic embellishments: *Damsels* and *Independents*. Wealth? there are not only Rich and Poor, there are: the poor, those who scrape by, those who have just enough, the comfortable, and the rich. Of course, for anyone with the contrary mania, tolerant neither of number nor of classification nor of system (numerous in Civilization, jealous of "spontaneity," of "life," of "imagination," etc.), the Fourierist Harmony would be hell itself: at thesis meals (contest meals), every course would have two labels, written in large letters, visible from afar and set on pivots, in both directions, "so that one can be read from across the table and the other the length of the table" (the present author has experienced a minor hell of this sort—but the system came from a French brain: in the American college where he took his meals, in order that the students might converse profitably while eating, and that they might benefit equally from the professor's lively discourse, each diner was supposed to advance one place at each meal, moving closer to the professorial sun, "in a clockwise direction," as the rule stated; there is little need to say that no "conversation" resulted from this astral movement).

Perhaps the *imagination of detail* is what specifically defines Utopia (opposed to political science); this would be logical, since detail is fantasmatic and thereby achieves the very pleasure of Desire. In Fourier, the number is rarely statistical (designed to assert averages, probabilities); it is, through the apparent finesse of its precision, essentially quantitative. Nuance, the game being stalked in this taxinomic hunting expedition, is a guarantee of pleasure (of fulfillment), since it determines a *just* combinative (knowing with whom to group ourselves in order to achieve complementarity with our own differences). Harmony must thus admit the operators of nuances, just as a tapestry workshop has specialists who are detailed to knot the threads. These nuance makers are: either operations (in Fourierist erotics, the "simple salute" is a preambular bacchanalia, a scrimmage enabling the partners to test each other before making a choice; during it, "trial caresses or reconnoiterings of the terrain" are practiced; this takes about eight minutes), or they are agents: there are: either "confessors" (these confessors do not hear any Fault: they "psychoanalyze" in order to elicit sympathies, often hidden by the subjects' appearance and ignorance: they are the decipherers of complementary nuances) or "dissolvents" (dissolvents, introjected into a group that has not yet found its just combinative, its "harmony," produce tremendous effects on it: they undo erroneous couplings by revealing to each his passions, they are transferers, mutators: thus lesbians and pederasts, who, thrown into the scrimmage, first accost the "champions of their own ilk," "recognize their own kind and sunder a good number of couples whom chance had united").

Nuance, the acme of number and of classification, has the *integral soul* as its total field, a human space defined by its amplitude, since it is the combinative dimension within which meaning is possible; no man is self-sufficient, no one his own integral soul: we need 810 characters of both sexes, or 1,620, to which are added the omnititles (the complex degree of contrasts) and the infinitesimal nuances of passion. The integral soul, a tapestry in which each nuance finds utterance, is the great sentence being sung by the universe: it is, in sum, the Language of which each of us is but a word. The Language is immortal: "At the era of the planet's death, its great soul, and consequently ours, inherent in it, will pass on to another, new sphere, to a planet which will be implaned, concentrated, saturated . . ."

The Nectarine

In any classification of Fourier, there is always a portion that is reserved. This portion has various names: passage, composite, transition, neuter, triviality, ambiguity (we might call it: *supplement*); naturally, it has a number: it is the ⅛ of any collection. First, this ⅛ has a function, familiar to scientists: it is the legal margin of error. ("Calculations of Attraction and Social Mobility are all subject to the ⅛ exception . . . it will always be understood.") Only, since in Fourier it is always a question of the *calculation of happiness,* error is at once ethical: when (abhorrent) Civilization "makes a mistake" (in its own system), it produces happiness: in Civilization, the ⅛ thus represents happy people. It is easy from this example to see that for Fourier the ⅛ portion does not derive from a liberal or statistical concession, from the vague recognition of a possible *deviation,* from a "human" failing in the system (to be taken philosophically); quite the contrary, it is a question of an important structural function, of a code constraint. Which one?

As a classifier (a taxinomist), what Fourier needs most are passages, special terms that permit making transitions (meshing) from one class to another,[13] the kind of lubricator the combinatory apparatus must use so as not to creak; the reserved portion is thus that of Transitions or Neuters (the neuter is what comes *between* the mark and the non-mark, this sort of buffer, damper, whose role is to muffle, to soften, to fluidify the semantic *tick-tock,* that metronome-like noise the paradigmatic alternative obsessively produces: *yes/no, yes/no, yes/no,* etc.). The nectarine, which is one of these Transitions, damps the opposition of prune and peach, as the quince damps that of pear and apple: they belong to the ⅛ of fruits. This portion (⅛) is shocking because it is contradictory: it is the class in which everything that attempts to escape classification is swallowed up; however, this portion is also superior: the space of the Neuter, of the *supplement of classification,* it joins realms, passions, characters; the art of employing Transitions is the major art of Harmonian cal-

[13] "Transitions are to passionate equilibrium what bolts and joints are to a framework."

culation: the neuter principle is controlled by mathematics, the pure language of the combinative, of the composed, the very badge of the *game*.

There are ambiguities in every series: the sensitive, the bat, the flying fish, the amphibians, the zoophytes, sapphism, pederasty, incest, Chinese society (half barbaric, half civilized, with harems and courts of law and etiquette), lime (fire and water), the nervous system (body and soul), twilights, coffee (ignominiously ignored at Mocha for 4,000 years, then suddenly the subject of a mercantile craze, passing from abjection to the highest rank), children (the third passionate sex, neither men nor women). Transition (mixed, Ambiguous, Neuter) is everything that is contrary duplicity, junction of extremes, and hence it takes as its emblematic form the ellipse, which has a double focus.

In Harmony, Transitions have a beneficent role; for example, they prevent monotony in love, despotism in politics: the distributive passions (composite, cabalistic, and butterfly) have a transitional role (they "mesh," ensure changes of "objects"); Fourier always reasoned contrariwise, what is beneficent in Harmony necessarily proceeds from what is discredited or rejected in Civilization: thus Transitions are "trivialities," ignored by civilized scholars as unworthy subjects: the bat, the albino, ugly ambiguous race, the taste for feathered fowl. The prime example of Trivial Transition is Death: transition ascending between Harmonian life and the happiness of the other life (sensual happiness), it "will shed all its odiousness when philosophy deigns to consent to study the transitions it proscribes as trivial." Everything rejected in Civilization, from pederasty to Death, has in Harmony a value that is eminent (but not pre-eminent: nothing dominates anything else, everything combines, meshes, alternates, revolves). This functional *justness* (this *justice*) is ensured by the ⅛ error. Thus, the *Neuter* is in opposition to the *Median;* the latter is a quantitative, not a structural, notion;

it is the amount of the oppression to which the large number
subjects the small number; caught in a statistical calculation,
the intermediate swells up and engulfs the system (thus the
middle class): the neuter, on the other hand, is a purely
qualitative, structural notion; it is what *confuses* meaning, the
norm, normality. To enjoy the *neuter* is perforce to be dis-
gusted by the *average*.

System/Systematics

". . . that the real content of these systems is hardly to be
found in their systematic form is best proved by the orthodox Fourierists . . . who, despite their orthodoxy, are the
exact antipodes of Fourier: doctrinaire bourgeois."

Marx and Engels, *German Ideology*

Fourier perhaps enables us to restate the following opposition (which we lately stated by distinguishing the novelistic
from the novel, poetry from the poem, the essay from the dissertation, the writing from the style, production from the
product, structuration from the structure[14]): the *system* is
a body of doctrine within which the elements (principles,
facts, consequences) develop logically, i.e., from the point of
view of the discourse, rhetorically. The system being a closed
(or monosemic) one, it is always theological, dogmatic; it is
nourished by illusions: an illusion of transparency (the language employed to express it is purportedly purely instrumental, it is not a writing) and an illusion of reality (the goal of
the system is to be *applied,* i.e., that it leave the language in
order to found a reality that is incorrectly defined as the ex-
teriority of language); it is a strictly paranoid insanity whose
path of transmission is insistence, repetition, cathechism,
orthodoxy. Fourier's work does not constitute a *system;* only
when we have tried to "realize" this work (in phalansteries)
has it become, retrospectively, a "system" doomed to instant

[14] *S/Z* (New York: Hill & Wang, 1974), p. 5.

fiasco; system, in the terminology of Marx and Engels, is the "systematic form," i.e., pure ideology, ideological reflection; *systematics* is the play of the system; it is language that is open, infinite, free from any referential illusion (pretension); its mode of appearance, its constituency, is not "development" but pulverization, dissemination (the gold dust of the signifier); it is a discourse without "object" (it only speaks of a thing obliquely, by approaching it indirectly: thus Civilization in Fourier) and without "subject" (in writing, the author does not allow himself to be involved in the imaginary subject, for he "performs" his enunciatory role in such a manner that we cannot decide whether it is serious or parody). It is a vast madness which does not end, but which permutates. In contrast to the system, monological, systematics is dialogical (it is the operation of ambiguities, it does not suffer contradictions); it is a writing, it has the latter's eternity (the perpetual permutation of meanings throughout History); systematics is not concerned with application (save as purist imagining, a theater of the discourse), but with transmission, (significant) circulation; further, it is transmittable only on condition it is *deformed* (by the reader); in the terminology of Marx and Engels, systematics would be the *real contents* (of Fourier). Here, we are not explaining Fourier's system (that portion of his systematics that plays with the system in an image-making way), we are talking solely about the several sites in his discourse that belong to systematics.

(Fourier puts the system to flight—cuts it adrift—by two operations: first, by incessantly delaying the definitive exposé until later: the doctrine is simultaneously highhanded and dilatory; next, by inscribing the system in the systematics, as dubious parody, shadow, game. For example, Fourier attacks the civilized [repressive] "system," he calls for an integral freedom [of tastes, passions, manias, whims]; thus, we would expect a spontaneistic philosophy, but we get quite the

opposite: a wild system, whose very excess, whose fantastic
tension, goes beyond system and attains systematics, i.e.,
writing: liberty is never the opposite of order, it is *order para-
grammatized:* the writing must simultaneously mobilize an
image and its opposite.)

The Party

What is a "party"? (1) *a partitioning,* isolating one group
from another, (2) an orgy, or *partouze,* as we say in French,
wherein the participants are linked erotically, and (3) a hand,
or *partie,* the regulated moment in a game, a collective diver-
sion. In Sade, in Fourier, the party, the highest form of societary or Sadian happiness, has this threefold character: it is
a worldly ceremony, an erotic practice, a social act.

Fourierist life is one immense party. At three-thirty in the
morning on the summer solstice (little sleep is needed in
Harmony), societary man is ready for the world: engaged in
a succession of "roles" (each one being the naked affirmation
of a passion) and subject to the combinative (meshing) rules
of these roles: this very exactly is the definition of mundanity,
which functions like a language: the mundane man is someone who spends his time *citing* (and in *weaving* what he
cites). The citations Fourier employs in blissfully describing
the worldly life of societary man are drawn paradoxically
(paragrammatically) from the repressive lexicons of the
Civilized regime: the Church, State, Army, Stock Exchange,
Salons, the penitentiary colony, and Scouting furnish the
Fourierist party with its most felicitous images.[15]

[15] Innumerable locutions, such as: "Saints and Patrons beatified and
canonized in the council of the Spheric Hierarchy." "Every pivotal
sin is liable to a sevenfold reparation" (VII, 191)—true, that this
reparation is hardly penitential, consisting as it does of making love
seven times with seven different people. "The Official Journal of
Gastromonic Transactions of the Army of the Euphrates" (VII, 378),
etc.

All mundanity is dissociative: it is a matter of isolating oneself in order to retreat and to trace out the area within which the rules of the game can function. The Fourierist party has two traditional enclosures, that of time and that of place.

The topography of the phalanstery traces an original site which is broadly that of palaces, monasteries, manors, and great blocks of buildings in which are mingled an organization of the building and an organization of territory, so that (a very modern viewpoint) architecture and urbanism reciprocally withdraw in favor of an over-all science of human space, the primary characteristic of which is no longer protection, but movement: the phalanstery is a retreat within which one moves (however, trips are taken outside the phalanstery: great mass excursions, ambulatory "parties"). Obviously, this space is functionalized, as shown in the following reconstruction (very approximate, since Fourierist discourse, like all writing, is irreducible).

The greatest concern of this organization is communication. Like the adolescent groups who live together during their summer vacations with constant pleasure and regretfully return home in the evenings, the societaries have only a temporary place for undressing and sleeping, warmed only by a brazier. In contrast, Fourier describes with great predilection and insistence the covered, heated, ventilated galleries, sanded basements, and corridors raised on columns that connect the palaces or manors of neighboring Tribes. A private place is allowed solely for lovemaking, and even this is only so that the unions made during the bacchanalias, get-togethers, or meetings for the purpose of selecting a companion, can be consummated—or "sealed."

Corresponding to topographical delimitation is this apparatus for temporal enclosure called *timing;* since a passion (for investments, for objects) must be changed every two hours, the optimal time is a divided time (the function of *timing* is to demultiply duration, to superproduce time and

PEACEFUL PURSUITS

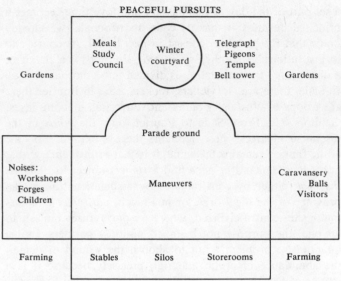

Gardens

Meals
Study
Council

Winter
courtyard

Telegraph
Pigeons
Temple
Bell tower

Gardens

Parade ground

Noises:
Workshops
Forges
Children

Maneuvers

Caravansery
Balls
Visitors

Farming

Stables

Silos

Storerooms

Farming

There are three stories, children on mezzanine

thereby to augment life power: "The day will never be long enough for the intrigues and merry reunions produced by the new order": we might be listening to an adolescent who, on vacation, has discovered his "group"); for example, in the combined Order there are five meals (at 5 A.M., the matutinal or "eye opener," at 8 A.M., lunch, dinner at 1, snack at 6, and supper at 9), and two collations (at 10 and 4): reminiscent of the schedule in an old-fashioned sanatorium. Harmonian man—physiologically regenerated by a diet of happiness—sleeps only from 11 in the evening to 3:30 in the morning; he never makes love at night, a detestable Civilized habit.

Love (erotic happiness, including the sentimental *eros*) is the main business of the long Harmonian day: "In Harmony, where no one is poor and where everyone is acceptable for lovemaking until a very advanced age, everyone devotes a set part of the day to this passion and love thus becomes a principal business: it has its code, its tribunals [we already know that the penalties consist in new loves], its court, and its institutions." Like the Sadian *eros,* Fourier's is a classifier, a distributor: the population is divided into amorous classes. In Sade, there are storytellers, fuckers, etc.; in Fourier there are troops of Vestals, Youths and Favorites of both sexes, Genitors, etc. From Sade to Fourier, only the *ethos* of the discourse changes: here jubilant, there euphoric. For the erotic fantasy remains the same; it is that of *availability:* that every love demand *at once* find a subject-object to be *at its disposal,* either by constraint or by association; this is the province of the ideal orgy, or in French, *partouze,* a fantasmatic site, contra-civilized, where no one refuses himself to anyone, the purpose not being to multiply partners (not a quantitative problem!) but to abolish the wound of denial; the abundance of erotic material, precisely because it is a matter of Desire and not of Need, is not intended to constitute a "consumer society" of love, but, paradox, truly utopian scandal, to make Desire function in its contradiction, namely: to fulfill *perpetually* (*perpetually* meaning simultaneously *always* and *never* fulfilled; or: *never and always:* that depends on the degree of enthusiasm or bitterness in which the fantasy is concluded). This is the sense of the supreme amorous institution of Fourierist society: the Angelicate (another ecclesiastical citation): in Harmony, the Angelicate is this handsome couple who, through "philanthropy," properly give themselves to any man or woman desiring them (including the deformed). The Angelicate has an additional function, not philanthropic but mediatory: it *conducts* desire: as though, left on his own, every man were incapable of knowing whom to desire, as though he were blind, powerless to invent his desire, as though it were always up to others to show us *where the desirable is* (clearly not the principal function of so-called erotic representations in mass culture: conduction, not substitution); the Angelic couple is the apex of the

amorous triangle: it is the vanishing point without which
there can be no erotic *perspective.*[16]
The party, a ritual common in Sade and in Fourier, has as
its "proof" a fact of the discourse which is to be found in
both: the amorous practice cannot be uttered save in the form
of a "scene," a "scenario," a "tableau vivant" (a strictly
fantasmatic disposition): the Sadian "séances" which often
even have a "setting": gardens, woods, colored veils, garlands of flowers, in Fourier the Cnidian novel. In fact, they
are part of the very force of fantasy, of the destructive power
it has over cultural models by using them *disrespectfully,* of
"representing" the erotic scene in the most insipid colors and
with the "proper" tone of petit-bourgeois art: Sade's most
shocking scenes, Fourier's pro-sapphic ravings, occur in a
Folies-Bergère setting: a carnival-like conjunction of transgression and opera, the sober site of mad acts, where the
subject is swallowed up in its culture, a decision that simultaneously sweeps away art and sex, denies transgression itself
any gravity, prohibits its ritualization (by providing for widespread prostitution the stage setting of *The Pearl Fishers*), the
headlong flight of the signified across the shifting of aesthetics
or sex, which ordinary language tries to achieve in its fashion
when it speaks (in French) of *ballets roses* and *ballets bleus*
("performances" by girls [pink] or boys [blue] "danced" before older men).

Compotes

An Eastern book says there is no better remedy for thirst
than a little cold compote, well sweetened, followed by a few
swallows of cool water. Fourier would have been doubly

[16] Can a more Sadian classification be imagined than the following:
the Angelicate is organized along three degrees of novitiate: (1)
cherubic (the postulant must sacrifice an entire day to each member of
the venerable choir); (2) *seraphic* (the sacrifice lasts several days and
is offered to both sexes); (3) *sayidic* (the sacrifice is offered up to a
chorus of patriarchs: probably even older!).

enchanted at this advice: first, because of the conjunction of
solid and liquid (the exemplar of a Transition, a Mix, a
Neuter, a Passage, a Twilight); next, because of its promotion
of compotes to the status of a philosophical food (the *Com-*
pound, not the Simple, slakes thirst, desire).

Harmony will be sweet. Why? For many reasons, constructed in superdetermination (the likely index of a fantasy)
First because sugar is an *anti-bread;* since bread is a mystic
object of Civilization, the symbol of labor and bitterness, the
emblem of Need, Harmony will invert the use of bread and
turn it into the colophon of Desire; bread will become a luxury food ("one of the most costly and most husbanded vic-
tuals"); in contrast, sugar will become wheat.[17] Next, because
sugar, hereby promoted, mixed with fruit in a compote, will
form the bread of Harmony, the basic nourishment of those
who have become wealthy and happy.[18] In a way, all Harmony has grown out of Fourier's taste for compotes, as a
man's desire can grow out of a child's dream (here the dream
of Candyland, of lakes of jam, of chocolate mountains): the
opus turns the far-off fantasy into sense: an entire construct
with immense, subtle ramifications (the societary regime, the
cosmogony of the new world) grows out of the etymological
metaphor: the compote (*composita*) being a composite, a
euphoric system of the Mixed is built up; for example: is a
hyperglycemic diet dangerous to health? Fourier is quick to
invent a counter-sugar, itself often highly sugared: "There
will be no drawbacks to this abundance of sweets when we

[17] "Then Africa will cheaply furnish the commodities of its hot
climate, cane sugar, which, pound for pound, will have the value of
wheat, when it is cultivated by 70 million Africans and all the peoples
of the Torrid Zone" (II, 14).

[18] "Then compotes made up of one-fourth sugar will be lavished on
children, because an equal measure of it will be cheaper than
bread . . . ; man's pivotal nourishment must not be bread, a simple
victual derived from one zone, but sugared fruit, a composed victual
allying the produce of two zones" (IV, 19).

can counterbalance sugar's wormy influence with a great abundance of alcoholic wines for men, white wines for women and children, acid beverages like lemonade, tart cedar . . ." Or rather: on the carrousel of the signifier, no one can say *what comes first,* Fourier's taste (for sugar, the negation of anything conflictual? for mixed fruits? for cooked food transformed into a semi-liquid consistency?) or the exaltation of a pure form, the composite-compote, the combinative. The signifier (Fourier is in full accord) is a non-originated, non-determined material, a text.

The Weather

Antique rhetoric, especially the medieval, included a special topic, the *impossibilia* (*adunata* in Greek); the *adunaton* was a common site, a *topos,* based on the notion of an *overabundance:* two naturally opposite, enemy elements (vulture and dove) were presented as peacefully living together ("The fire burns within the ice / The sun grows dark / I see the moon about to fall / This tree moves from its place," wrote Théophile de Viau); the impossible image served to stigmatize a hateful tense, a shocking *contra-naturam* ("We will have seen everything!"). Once again, Fourier inverts the rhetorical site; he uses the *adunaton* to celebrate the marvels of Harmony, the conquest of Nature by contra-natural means; for example, nothing is more incontestably "natural" (eternal) than the brackishness of the sea, whose water is undrinkable; Fourier, by the aromal action of the North Polar cap, turns it to lemonade (tart cedar): a positive *adunaton.*

Fourier's *adunata* are many. They can all be reduced to the (very modern) conviction that man's farming modifies the climate.[19] For Fourier, human "nature" is not deformable

[19] ". . . the air is a field, subject as is the earth to industrious exploitation" (III, 97).

(merely combinable), but "natural" nature is modifiable (the reason being that Fourier's cosmogony is *aromal,* tied to the notion of the sexual fluid, whereas his psychology is discontinuous, dedicated to arrangement, not to effluvium. This *topos* of the *impossible* abides by the categories of antique rhetoric:

I.   *Chronographies* (temporal impossibilities): "We shall be witness to a spectacle to be seen once on each globe: the sudden passage from incoherence to social combination. . . . During this metamorphosis, each year will equal a century of existence," etc.

II.   *Topographies:* Spatial impossibilities, very numerous, arise from what we call geography: (1) *Climatology:* (a) Fourier changes climates, makes the Pole into a new Andalusia and moves the pleasant temperature of Naples and Provence to the coast of Siberia; (b) Fourier improves the seasons, hateful in civilized France (theme: *Spring has fled!*): "1822 had no winter, 1823 no spring at all. This confusion, which has gone on for ten years, is the result of an aromal lesion the planet is suffering because of the undue duration of chaos, civilized, barbarous and savage" (theme: *It's because of the Bomb*); (c) Fourier orders micro-climates: "The atmosphere and its protection are an integral part of our clothing. . . . In Civilization, no one ever dreamed of improving that part of the clothing we call atmosphere, with which we are perpetually in contact" (the theme of the phalanstery's corridors, heated and ventilated). (2) *Podology:* "[Crusaders of old shoes] . . . are carried off en masse to Jerusalem and brought out to cover over with good soil and plantations that Calvary where the Christians come to recite useless Our Father's; in three days, a fertile mountain has been created. Thus their religion consists in usefulness and agreeableness toward those countries to which our stupid piety brought only ravage and superstition." (3) *Physical Geography:* Fourier subjects the map of the world to a veritable plastic surgery:

he moves continents, grafts climates, "lifts" South America (as we lift breasts), "lowers" Africa, pierces isthmuses (Suez and Panama), permutates cities (Stockholm is put in the place of Bordeaux, St. Petersburg of Turin), makes Constantinople the capital of the Harmonian world. (4) *Astronomy:* "Man is called upon to displace and replace the stars."

III.   *Prosographies:* modifications of the human body: (a) *Stature:* "Mankind's height will increase 2 to 3 inches per generation, until it has attained the average of 84 inches or 7 feet for men." (b) *Age:* "Then the full span of life will be 144 years and vigor proportionate." (c) *Physiology:* "This multitude of meals is necessary for the ravenous appetite the New Order will create. . . . Children raised in this way will acquire iron temperaments and will be subject to a renewal of appetite every 2 or 3 hours, due to the speedy digestion that will result from the delicacy of the food" (here again we touch on a Sadian theme: what in Fourier is the regulation of indigestion by digestion becomes inverted [or set right] in Sade, where indigestion rules the digestion —coprophagy requires good fecal matter). (d) *Sex:* "In order to confound the tyranny of men there must have existed for a century a third sex, male and female, stronger than man."

It is nugatory to stress the reasonable nature of these ravings, because certain of them are being implemented (acceleration of History, the modification of climate through agriculture or urbanization, the piercing of isthmuses, the transformations of soils, the conversion of desert sites into cultivated sites, the conquest of the heavenly bodies, the increase in longevity, the physical improvement of the race). The most insane (the most resistant) *adunaton* is not the one that upsets the laws of "nature," but the one that upsets the laws of language. Neologisms are Fourier's *impossibilia*. It is easier to predict the subversion of "the weather" than to imagine, as does Fourier, a masculine form of a feminine

word, *Fés* for *Fées:* the upheaval of a strange graphic con-
figuration in which femininity has been sunk, there is the true
impossible: the impossible garnered from sex and language:
in "*matrones* (feminine) and *matrons* (masculine)," a new,
monstrous, transgressor *object* has come to mankind.

SADE II

Hiding the Woman

IN THEIR PLEASURES, all libertines have an overwhelming urge to hide the Female's sexual organs scrupulously. Threefold profit. First, morality is overturned by a derisory parody: the same sentence serves both libertine and puritan: "Conceal your cunts, ladies," an indignant Gernande says to Juliette and Dorothée, in the same tone that Tartuffe uses in addressing Dorine ("Cover that breast so that I do not see it"); sentence and clothing remain in place, but for opposite ends, here hypocritical modesty, there debauchery. Does the best of subversions not consist in disfiguring codes, not in destroying them?

Next: Woman is destroyed: she is wrapped up, twisted about, veiled, disguised so as to erase every trace of her anterior features (figure, breasts, sexual organs); a kind of surgical and functional doll is produced, a body *without a front part* (structural horror and flouting), a monstrous bandage, a *thing*.

Finally, in his order of occultation, the libertine contradicts everyday immorality; he takes the opposite tack from sophomoric pornography, which makes the supreme audacity the sexual denudation of Woman. Sade calls for a *counter-strip-tease;* whereas on the music-hall stage, the diamond triangle which ultimately resists the dancer's undressing designates, by making it forbidden, the very arcana of bliss, in the libertine ceremony this same triangle defines a site of horror:

"Bressac places triangular handkerchiefs, tied at the loins, and the two women advance . . ."

Libertine morality consists not in destroying but in diverting; it diverts the object, the word, the organ from its endoxal usage; however, for this theft to occur, for the libertine system to prevaricate at the expense of common morality, the meaning must persist, Woman must contrive to represent a paradigmatic area, with two sites, one of which the libertine, a linguist respectful of the sign, will mark, and the other which he will neutralize. Of course, by concealing the Female's sexual organs, by baring her buttocks, the libertine seems to be making her into a boy and seeking in Woman what is not Woman; however, the scrupulous abolition of difference is a trick, for this asexual Woman is still not the Other of Woman (the boy): among the subjects of debauchery, Woman remains pre-eminent (pederasts, who are usually loath to recognize Sade as one of theirs, are not mistaken); the paradigm must function; only Woman offers the choice of two sites of intromission: in choosing one over the other *in the area of the same body,* the libertine produces and assumes a meaning, that of transgression. The boy, because his body provides the libertine with no opportunity for stating the paradigm of sites (he offers but one), is less *forbidden* than Woman: thus, systematically, he is less interesting.

Food

Sadian food is functional, systematic. This is not enough to make it novelistic. Sade adds to it a supplementary utterance: the invention of detail, the naming of dishes. Victorine, the overseer of Sainte-Marie-des-Bois, eats for her meal a truffled turkey, a Périgueux pâté, a Bolognese mortadella, and drinks six bottles of champagne; elsewhere, Sade notes the menu of "a highly irritating dinner: soup made from the stock of twenty-four small sparrows with rice and saffron, a pie stuffed with chopped pigeon and garnished with artichoke bottoms, eggs, ambergris compote." The passage from generic notation ("they eat") to the detailed menu ("at dawn they were served scrambled eggs, chincara, onion soup, and omelettes") constitutes the very mark of the novelistic: we could classify novels according to the frankness of their alimentary allusions: in Proust, Zola, Flaubert, we always know what the characters eat; in Fromentin, Laclos, or even Stendhal, we do not. The alimentary detail goes beyond signification, it is the enigmatic supplement of meaning (of ideology); in the goose the aged Galileo stuffs down there is not only an active symbol of the situation (Galileo is out of things; he eats; his books must act for him), but also something like a Brechtian tenderness for bliss. Likewise, Sade's menus have the (non-functional) function of introducing pleasure (and not only merely transgression) into the libertine world.

The Conveyor Belt

The Sadian Eros is obviously sterile (diatribes against reproduction). His model, however, is labor. The orgy is organized, distributed, ordered, and supervised like a studio sitting; its profitability is of the assembly line (but without a survalue): "In all my days," Juliette says, sodomized 300 times in two hours at Francaville's, "I have never seen a service so smartly done as that. The handsome members, once ready, were passed on from hand to hand, down to the children who were to insert them; they disappeared into the patient's ass hole; they emerged, they were replaced; and all done with an address, an alacrity impossible to describe." What is being described here is in fact a machine (the Machine is the sublimated emblem of labor insofar as it simultaneously accomplishes and exonerates); children, Ganymedes, preparers, everyone creates an immense and subtle mechanism, a meticulous clockwork, whose function is to connect the sexual discharges, to produce a continuous tempo, to bring pleasure to the subject on a conveyor belt (the subject is magnified as the outcome and final point of the entire machinery, and yet denied, reduced to a part of his body). Every combinative needs an operator for continuity; now the simultaneous covering of every bodily site, now, as here, the rapidity of the obturations.

Censorship, Invention

Sade is apparently doubly censured: when, in one way or another, the sale of his books is banned; when he is declared to be boring, unreadable. Yet true censorship, the ultimate censorship, does not consist in banning (in abridgment, in suppression, in deprivation), but in unduly fostering, in maintaining, retaining, stifling, getting bogged down in (intellectual, novelistic, erotic) stereotypes, in taking for nourishment only the received word of others, the repetitious matter of common opinion. The real instrument of censorship is not the police, it is the *endoxa*. Just as a language is better defined by what it obliges to be said (its obligatory rubrics) than by what it forbids to be said (its rhetorical rules), so social censorship is not found where speech is hindered, but where it is constrained.

The ultimate subversion (contra-censorship) does not necessarily consist in saying what shocks public opinion, morality, the law, the police, but in inventing a paradoxical (pure of any *doxa*) discourse: *invention* (and not provocation) is a revolutionary act: it cannot be accomplished other than in setting up a new language. Sade's greatness lies not in having celebrated crime, perversion, nor in having employed in this celebration a radical language; it is in having invented a vast discourse founded in its own repetitions (and not those of others), paid out in details, surprises, voyages, menus, portraits, configurations, proper nouns, etc.: in short, contra-censorship, from the forbidden, becomes the novelistic.

Hatred of Bread

Sade does not like bread. The reason is doubly political. On the one hand, Bread is the emblem of virtue, religion, labor, difficulty, need, poverty, and it must be despised as a *moral* object; on the other hand, it is a means of blackmail: tyrants subject the people by threatening to take away their bread; it is a symbol of oppression. Sadian bread, therefore, is a contradictory sign: moral and immoral, condemned in the first instance by the contestatory Sade and in the second by the revolutionary Sade.

Yet the text cannot stop at the ideological (though contradictory) meaning: to the Christian's bread and the tyrant's bread is added a third bread, a "textual" bread; this bread is a "pestilential amalgamation of flour and water"; a substance, it is taken into the properly Sadian system, the body; it is removed from the diet of harems because it would produce in the subjects digestions unfitting for coprophagy. Thus the meaning turns round: a carrousel of determinations which stops nowhere and of which the text is the perpetual motion.

The Lit Body

Sade, no more than anyone else, cannot succeed in describing beauty; at the most, he can affirm it by means of cultural references ("made like Venus," "the shape of Minerva," "the freshness of Flora"). Being analytical, language can come to grips with the body only if it cuts it up; the total body is outside language, only pieces of the body succeed to writing; in order to *make* a body *seen,* it must either be displaced, refracted through the metonymy of clothing, or reduced to one of its parts; now the description becomes visionary, the felicity of the utterance is re-established (perhaps because there exists a fetish vocation of language): the monk Severino finds in Justine "a decided superiority in the shape of her buttocks, a warmth, an inexpressible tightness in her anus." Just as the bodies of Sadian subjects are insipid, since they are totally beautiful (beauty is only a *class*), so the buttocks, the breath, the sperm find an immediate individuality of language. However, there is a way of giving these insipid and perfect bodies a textual existence. This way is the theater (as the author of these lines understood when he attended one evening a drag performance in a Parisian nightclub). Captured in its insipidness, its abstraction ("the most sublime bosom, very pretty details in the forms, disengagement of masses, grace, softness in the articulation of members," etc.), the Sadian body is in fact a body seen from a distance in the full light of the stage; it is merely a *very well lit* body the very illumination of which, even, distant, effaces individuality (skin blemishes, ill-favored complexion), but allows the pure charm to come through; totally desirable and absolutely inaccessible, the lit body has as its natural arena the intimate theater, the nightclub, the fantasy, or the Sadian presentation (the Sadian victim's body does not become accessible until it leaves its first description and is broken up). Finally, it is this abstract body's theatricality which is rendered in dull expressions (*perfect body, ravishing body, fit for a painting,* etc.), as though the description of the body had been exhausted by its (implicit) staging: perhaps it is the function of this touch of hysteria which underlies all theater (all lighting) to combat this touch of fetishism contained in the very "cutting" of the written sentence. However that may be, I had only to experience a vivid emotion in the presence of the lit bodies in the Parisian nightclub for the (apparently very tame) allusions Sade makes to the beauty of his subjects to cease to bore me and to glitter in their turn with all the illumination and intelligence of desire.

Inundation

Juliette, Olympe, and Clairwil are dealing with ten fishermen of Baiae; since there are three ladies, three fishermen are satisfied straightaway, but the remainder begin to quarrel; Juliette calms them down by demonstrating for them that with a little art each of the three women can occupy three men (the tenth, exhausted, will be content to watch). This art is that of catalysis: it consists in saturating the erotic body by simultaneously occupying the principal sites of pleasure (mouth, sexual organs, anus); each subject is thrice fulfilled (in both meanings of the word) and hence each of the nine partners finds his erotic employment (true, this employment is simple, whereas the subjects' pleasure is three-fold; class difference: libertines as against agents, rich adventuresses as against poor fishermen).

The principle of Sadian eroticism is the saturation of every area of the body: one tries to employ (to occupy) every separate part. This is the same problem the sentence faces (in which respect we have to speak of a Sadian erotography, there being no distinction between the structure of ejaculation and that of language): the (literary, written) sentence is also a body to be catalyzed by filling all its principal sites (subject-verb-complement) with expansions, incidental clauses, subordinates, determinators: of course, this saturation is utopian, for nothing (structurally) permits terminating a sentence: we can always add to it that supplement which will never be the final one (this *uncertainty* of the sentence made Flaubert extremely unhappy); similarly, although Sade tries to prolong the inventory of erotic sites incessantly, he knows he cannot close the amorous body, terminate the voluptuous catalysis (finish it off), and exhaust the combinative of its units: there is always a supplement of demand, of desire, one tries illusively to exhaust, either by repeating or permutating the figures (accountancy of "acts"), or by crowning the combinative operation (analytical by definition) with an ecstatic feeling of continuity, covering, perfusion.

This combinative transcendency was also sought by the first theoretician of the sentence, Denys d'Halicarnasse: it was a matter of postulating a *diffuse* value, distributed over the addition and articulation of the words (a linked, rhythmic, respiratory value). Now, the passing from summationary catalysis to an existential totality is what achieves the Sadian body's *inundation* (by sperm, blood, excrement, vomit); a bodily mutation is thus achieved: other bodies "weigh upon" and "adhere to" this new body. The ultimate erotic state (analogous to the sublime legato of the phrase, which in music is called "phrasing") is *to swim:* in corporeal substances, delights, the deep feelings of lasciviousness. This entire erotic combinative, so inflexible in its painstaking discontinuity, finally leads to the levitation of the amorous body: as proved by the very impossibility of the figures suggested: to accomplish them, if they are taken literally, one would need a multiple and disarticulated body.

Social

Sadian adventures are not fabulous: they take place in a real world contemporary with the time of Sade's youth, i.e., the society of Louis XV. Sade strongly emphasizes the social armature of that world; the libertines belong to the aristocracy, or more exactly (and more frequently) to the class of financiers, professionals, and prevaricators, in short: exploiters, the majority made wealthy in Louis XV's wars and by the corrupt practices of despotism; unless their noble origin is a voluptuary factor (the rape of fashionable young ladies), the subjects belong to the industrial and urban subproletariat (the urchins of Marseilles, for example, children "who work in factories and provide the aged roués of that city with the prettiest objects one could hope to find") or serfs on feudal lands, where they subsist (in Sicily, for example, where Jérôme, the future monk in *Justine,* goes to live, according to an arcadian plan which will, he says, enable him to have dominion over both his lands and his vassals).

However, there is a paradox: class relationships in Sade are both brutal and indirect; uttered in line with the radical contrast between exploiters and exploited, these relationships do not come into the novel as though for referential description (as is the case with a great "social" novelist like Balzac);

Sade uses them differently, not as an image to be portrayed, but *as a model to be reproduced.* Where? In the libertine's small society; this society is constructed like a model, a miniature; Sade *transports* class division into it; on one side, the exploiters, the possessors, governors, tyrants; on the other, the *ordinary people.* The stimulus for the division (as in the larger society) is (sadistic) *profitability:* "One established . . . over the ordinary people every vexation, every injustice imaginable, certain that the greater the tyranny one exercised, the greater the sum of pleasures to be withdrawn." Between the social novel (Balzac read by Marx) and the Sadian novel, a kind of general to and fro maneuver then occurs: the social novel maintains social relationships in their original place (society as a whole) but anecdotizes them for the sake of individual biographies (César Birotteau, tradesman; Coupeau, zinc worker); the Sadian novel takes the *formula* of these relationships, but transports them elsewhere, into an artificial society (as did Brecht in *The Threepenny Opera*). In the first instance, we have *reproduction,* in the meaning that word has in painting, in photography; in the second instance, there is, one might say, *re-production,* repeated production of a practice (and not of an historical "picture"). The consequence is that the Sadian novel is more "real" than the social novel (which is realistic); the Sadian practices appear to us today to be totally improbable; however, we need only travel in any underdeveloped country (analogous, all in all, to eighteenth-century France) to understand that they are still operable there: the same social division, the same opportunities for recruitment, the same availability of subjects, the same conditions for seclusion, and the same impunity, so to speak.

Politeness

When Sade is working, he addresses himself in the polite *vous:* "Do not depart from this plan in any way. . . . Detail

the beginning . . . soften the first part . . . paint . . .
recapitulate carefully . . ." etc., all use the polite form of
the verb in French. Neither *I* nor the familiar *tu,* the subject
of the writing treats himself with the greatest distance, that of
the social code: this self-addressed politeness is a little as if
the subject were picking himself up with tweezers, or at least
surrounding himself with quotation marks: a supreme subversion which, by contrast, puts the systematic practice of
speaking in the familiar, saying *tu,* in its (conformist) place.

The remarkable thing is that this politeness, which is in no
way respect, but distance, is employed by Sade whenever
he finds himself in *a work situation, under the proceedings of
the writing.* Writing is *first* to place the subject (including his
written image-reservoir) under citation, to destroy any complicity, any importunity between the tracer and the inventor,
or better yet, between he who *has written* and he who (re)-
reads himself (as can be seen in the inadvertencies—in the
enumeration of victims, for example—against which Sade ad-
monishes himself).

Inserted into the blazing universe of libidinous practices,
politeness is not a class protocol, but more strongly that
imperious gesture of language by means of which the libertine or the writer or, let us say, the *pornographer,* he who
literally writes debauchery, imposes his own solitude and
rejects cordiality, complicity, solidarity, equality, the entire
morality of the human relationship, i.e., hysteria. La Duclos,
the storyteller of *The 120 Days,* who has just recounted a
hundred stories concerning excrement, has always *told them
correctly:* she regulates her language with exquisite arabesques of a Proustian preciosity ("A certain bell we will soon
hear shall convince me that I would not have had time to
finish the evening out," etc.); and within his most crude
orders, the libertine never forgets the distance due his colleagues and himself ("And you, madame, does watching suffering excite you?" " 'As you see, sir,' the tribade replies,

showing her fingertips covered with mung"): Sadian partners are neither comrades, chums, nor co-militants.

Rhetorical Figures

In Sade, libidinous practice is a true text—so that concerning it we must speak of *pornography,* which means: not the discourse being sustained on amorous acts, but this tissue of erotic figures, cut up and combined like rhetorical figures of the written discourse. In the scenes of sexual acts, we thus find configurations of characters, series of actions, strictly analogous to the "ornaments" collected and named by classical rhetoric. In the first place, *metaphor,* indiscriminately substituting one subject for another according to a single paradigm, that of vexation. Next, for example: *asyndeton,* a curt succession of debaucheries ("I committed parricide, I committed incest, I committed prostitution, I committed sodomy," Saint-Fond says, balancing units of crime like Caesar of conquest: *Veni, vidi, vici); anacoluthon,* a break in the construction by which the stylist flouts his grammar (*Had Cleopatra's nose been shorter . . .*) and the libertine erotic conjunctions ("Nothing amuses me like beginning in one ass hole the operation I want to finish in another"). And just as an audacious writer can create an outrageous stylistic figure, so Rombeau and Rodin endow erotic discourse with a new figure (penetrating rapidly and in turn the aligned posteriors of four girls), to which, good grammarians that they are, they do not neglect to give a name (*the windmill*).

Crudity

Sade's sexual lexicon (when "crude") has a linguistic prowess: it sticks to pure denotation (an exploit usually reserved for scientific, algorithmic languages); Sadian discourse seems to be constructed on a bedrock that nothing can penetrate, move, transform; it maintains a lexicographic

truth, Sade's (sexual) words are as pure as dictionary words
(the dictionary being that object one cannot mount up to
but only descend from. The dictionary represents the *limit*
of the language; to put oneself at that limit takes the same
audacity needed to go beyond it: a situational analogy
exists between the crude word and the new word: neologism
is an obscenity, and the sexual word, if direct, is always received as if it had never been read). Through the crudity of
the language a discourse *outside meaning* is established,
thwarting any "interpretation" and even any symbolism, a
custom-free territory exterior to the exchange and to the
penal system, a kind of Adamic language stubbornly determined not to signify: we might call it *language without
supplement* (the major utopia of poetry).

Yet Sadian discourse has a supplement: when it appears
that this language is *destined,* caught in a certain circuit of
destination, that connecting the practitioner of debauchery
(libertine or subject) to his image-creating speech, i.e., to
the (virtuous or criminal) justifications he gives himself:
to hold out one's hand for one's partner's turd is disgusting
in the victim's language, delightful in the libertine's language; thus the "local notions" (which make adultery, infanticide, sodomy, anthropophagy condemned here and
revered there) which Sade so frequently uses to justify
crime, are in fact language operators: that part of the language that reverses onto the utterance, like the meaning
itself, the particularity of its destination: the supplement
is the Other; however, as there is neither desire nor discourse
before the Other and outside the Other, Sade's crude language is the utopian portion of his discourse: a rare, coura-
geous utopia, not because it bares sexuality, nor even because
it naturalizes it, but because it appears to believe in the possibility of a subject-less lexicon (yet the Sadian text is reduced by the phenomenological return of the subject, the
author: the utterer of sadism).

Watered Silk

The (polychromatic) languages of the libertine and the (monotonal) language of the victim coexist with a thousand other Sadian languages: the cruel, the obscene, the ironic, the polite, the pointed, the didactic, the comic, the lyric, the novelistic, etc. A text is thus created which gives (as do few texts) the sensation of its etymology: it is a damask fabric, a tapestry of phrases, a changing luster, a fluctuating and glittering surface of styles, a watered silk of languages: a discursive plural uncommon in French literature is achieved (through heredity and classic constraint, the French are bored by the plural, they think they like only homogeneity, sublimated and praised as "unity of tone"—which is precisely, literally—*the monotone*). One other French author at least has played with these multiple changes of language: Proust, whose work is thereby relieved of any boredom; for as it is possible to distinguish several motifs in a calendared material, to isolate and follow one and ignore the others, one can according to one's mood read Sade, Proust, by "skipping," according to the moment, this or that of their languages (I can, on that day, read only Charlus's code, and not Albertine's, the Sadian dissertation and not the erotic scene); the plural of the text is based on the multiplicity of the codes, but it is ultimately achieved by the ease with which the reader can "ignore" certain pages, this ignoring somehow being prepared for and legalized beforehand by the author himself, who has taken pains to produce a *perforated* text so that anyone "skipping" the Sadian dissertations will stay within the truth of the Sadian text.

Impossibilia

In the scholastic game of *disputatio*, the respondent (the candidate) was sometimes asked to defend *impossibilia*,

apparently impossible theses. In the same manner, imagining
the attitudes of debauchery, Sade is defending "impossibilities." Indeed, if some group conceived the desire to realize
literally one of the orgies Sade describes (like the positivistic
doctor who crucified an actual cadaver in order to show that
the crucifixion described in the Gospels was anatomically
impossible, or in any case would not have produced the
painter's Christ on the Cross), the Sadian scene would
quickly be seen to be utterly unreal: the complexity of the
combinations, the partners' contortions, the potency of
ejaculations, and the victims' endurance all surpass human
nature: one would need several arms, several skins, the
body of an acrobat, and the ability to achieve orgasm *ad
infinitum*. Sade knew this, for he has someone say to
Juliette, standing before the frescoes in Herculaneum: "We
note . . . in all these paintings a luxury of poses almost
impossible in nature, evidencing either a great muscular
suppleness in the inhabitants of these lands, or a great disorder of the imagination." The anecdotal improbability is
even more marked: the victims (save for Justine) neither
protest nor struggle; they need not be mastered; in a retreat
where the four gentlemen of *The 120 Days* are alone, without help, without police or servants, no fucker, no Hercules
grabs a chair, a club, to knock out the libertine who has
condemned him to death. The only thing that can pass from
the Book into reality (why not test the "realism" of a work
by examining not the more or less exact way in which it
reproduces reality, but on the contrary the way in which
reality could or could not effectuate the novel's utterance?
Why shouldn't a book be programmatic, rather than painting?), the only thing that can constitute a sort of Sadian
Museum, is the tools of debauchery: the case of dildoes,
the voluptuary machines and Clairwil's drink, the topographical diagram of the orgiastic sites, etc.

For the rest, everything is left to the power of the discourse. This little-considered power is not merely evocative, but also negative. Language has this property of denying, ignoring, dissociating reality: when written, shit does not have an odor; Sade can inundate his partners in it, we receive not the slightest whiff, only the abstract sign of something unpleasant. So libertinage appears: a fact of language. Sade radically contrasts language with reality, or more precisely, he places himself at the sole instance of the "reality of language," and therefore he was able to write, proudly: "Yes, I am a libertine, I admit it: I have conceived all that can be conceived along that line, but I have certainly not done everything I have conceived and I shall certainly never do it. I am a libertine, but I am neither a criminal nor a murderer." "Reality" and the book are *cut apart:* they are not linked by any obligation: an author can talk about his work *ad infinitum,* he is never *bound* to guarantee it.

The Handkerchief

"What, madame, something is pushing that handkerchief aside? I thought I was disguising a cunt, merely, and I discover a cock? Fuck it! What a clitoris! Remove that veil . . ." The unspeakable thing is this feminine linen on *that.*

The Family

To transgress the familiar interdiction consists in altering the terminological distinctness of the parental pattern, to make only one signified (an individual, a girl called Olympe, for example) receive simultaneously several of these names, these signifiers that the institution elsewhere carefully keeps distinct, aseptically free from any confusion: "Olympe," says the incestuous monk of Sainte-Marie-des-Bois, "combines the threefold honor of being simultaneously my daughter, my granddaughter, and my niece." In other words, the crime consists in transgressing the semantic rule, in creating homonymy: the act *contra naturam* is exhausted in an utterance of counter-language, the family is no more than a lexical area, but this reduction is in no way immaterial: it guarantees the strongest of transgressions, that of language, its full outrage: to transgress is *to name outside the lexical division* (the basis of society, for the same reason as class division).

The Family is defined on two levels: its "content" (ties of affection, society, gratitude, respect, etc.), at which the libertine mocks, and its "form," the network of nominative ties—and therefore combinatory ties—with which the libertine plays, which he recognizes the better to fake them and on which he brings to bear syntactical operations; it is on this second level that for Sade the original transgression occurs, the one that produces the intoxication of a continuous invention, the jubilation of incessant surprises: "He says he knew a man who had fucked three children he had had with his mother, whence he had a daughter he had married to his son, so that by fucking her he was fucking his sister, his daughter, and his daughter-in-law, and he was making his son fuck his sister and his stepmother." Thus transgression appears as a nominative surprise: to posit that the son will be the spouse or husband (depending on whether the father, Noirceuil, sodomizes his progeny or is sodomized by it) fills Sade with the same wonder as that which seizes the Proustian Narrator when he discovers that the Guermantes' Way and Swann's Way come together: incest, like time recaptured, is only a surprise of vocabulary.

Mirrors

The Occident has made the mirror, always spoken of in the singular, the very symbol of narcissism (of I, of the refracted Unit, the reassembled Body). Mirrors (plural) is quite another theme, whether the mirrors are set up facing each other (Zen image) so as to reflect nothing but emptiness, or whether the multiplicity of juxtaposed mirrors sur-

rounds the objects with a circular image whereby coming and
going is eliminated. This is the case with Sadian mirrors.
The libertine enjoys performing his orgy amid reflections,
in niches lined with mirrors or in groups charged with repeating a single image: "The Italian is being buggered; four
naked women surround him on every side; the image he
adores is reproduced a thousand different ways before his
libertine eyes; he comes"; this latter disposition has the
dual advantage of identifying subjects with furniture
(Sadian theme: at Minski's, the tables and chairs are girls)
and of repeating the partial object, thereby covering, in-
undating the libertine with a luminous, fluid orgy. A criminal surface is thus created: the working area is *coated* with
debauchery.

The Blow

The language of debauchery is often *beaten out*. It is a
Cornelian, Caesarian language: " 'My friend,' I said to the
youth, 'you see all I have done for you; it is high time to
recompense me.' 'What is it you want?' 'Your ass.' 'My ass?'
'You shall not possess Euphrémie ere I have obtained my
demand.' " We might be listening to the aged Horace:
"What would you have had him do against three?" "Die!"
Thus, through Sade and thanks to him, rhetoric appears:
a machine for desire: there are language fantasms: con-
cision, contraction, detonation, fall, in short, the *blow* is
one of these fantasms (in French, to strike, *frapper,* applies to medals, counterfeit money, champagne, and young
toughs): it is the combustive *striking* of the inscription, the
orgasm that ends the sentence at the peak of its pleasure.

Rhapsody

Little studied by narrative grammarians (e.g., Propp),
there is a rhapsodic structure of narrative, especially proper
to the picaresque novel (and perhaps to the Proustian

novel). To recount, here, does not consist in developing
a story and then untangling it, adhering to an infinitely or-
ganic model (to be born, to live, to die), i.e., to subject the
series of episodes to a natural (or logical) order, which
becomes the meaning imposed by "Fate'" on every life,
every journey, but in purely and simply juxtaposing iterative
and mobile fragments: then the continuum is merely a series
of bits and pieces, a baroque fabric of odds and ends. The
Sadian rhapsody thus unfolds without order: voyages, thefts,
murders, philosophical dissertations, libidinous scenes, escapes, secondary narratives, schedules of orgies, descriptions of machines, etc. This construction frustrates the paradigmatic structure of the narrative (in which each episode
has its "correspondent" somewhere further on which coun-
terbalances or rectifies it) and thereby, eluding the struc-
turalist reading of the narration, it constitutes an outrage
of meaning: the rhapsodic (Sadian) novel has no *meaning* or *direction,* nothing compels it to progress, develop,
end.

The Furnishings of Debauchery

The orgy occurs in the handsomest of rooms, readied
in the morning by the old women:
The floor is an immense quilted mattress six inches
thick: a tendential conjunction of bed and flooring; civiliza-
tions where one goes barefoot in the bedroom, not to avoid
"dirtying" it—a petit-bourgeois scruple which in certain
apartments obliges visitors to put on a rather ridiculous
sort of slipper—but to achieve total intimacy, that of body
and the furnished surface, and thus to alleviate in advance
the censure created by the vertical, legal, moral, separative
stance; to stand upright is supposedly virile; a being shod is
a being who cannot *fall* (or can only fall); to remain shod
within an area means that pleasure is therein foreclosed (in
Japan, some Frenchmen dislike removing their shoes, either

for fear of losing their virility or because they are embarrassed at the hole in their stocking).

Two or three dozen squares (four-cornered cushions) are tossed onto this mattress: this is the custom today in a few "clubs" in which, at least on this point, vulgarity and morality have not been able completely to obliterate the meaning of *art de vivre*.

At the end of the room, a large ottoman is set, surrounded by mirrors: mirrors drown with images: in addition, in the old days, when a mirror cost many days of labor, it was the sign of great luxury, almost the emblematic product of exploitation (as today a yacht, a private plane).

Rolling tables, of ebony and porphyry, set here and there, hold all the accessories of libertinage (whips, condoms, dildoes, lubricants, perfumes, etc.); the séance of debauchery has all the protocol of a surgical operation; the debauché, wherever in the room he happens to be, must have the instruments of sensual pleasure within his reach; he rolls his little table around with him like a manicurist or a nurse (the debauchery is made dreadful by this small detail in the reading).

Opposite the ottoman, an enormous buffet offers throughout the day a profusion of foods that can be kept warm "imperceptibly"; in short, the salon of debauchery is a worldly salon; as in any bourgeois reception, there is, in the background, a standing buffet (the difference being that this buffet serves not to relieve one's boredom at one's neighbor's conversation, but to replenish loss of sperm and blood): this buffet *in the background* makes it a cocktail party.

There are great numbers of roses, carnations, lilies, jasmine, lilies of the valley; yet the debauchery will terminate in a sea of excrement and vomit; the flowers are inaugural; they establish the onset of a degradation that is a part of the libertine plan.

Across from the buffet, "artistically placed in a cloud," there is an effigy of the so-called God: a mechanical tableau in line with that period's liking for automata, for later on, according to a game that turns the debauchery into a lottery, the Eternal's mouth will emit rolls of white satin ribbon on which is written, *à la* Ten Commandments, the order for certain positions: "post office" is also played at this rout.

Sadian debauchery, usually referred to only as a function of the philosophical system of which it is no more than the abstract cipher, in fact participates in an *art de vivre:* in it is inscribed the concomitance of the pleasures.

The Mark

The subjects are marked (with different colors) at the Château of Silling. The purpose of this mark is each victim's deflowering, reserved to one or another of the four Gentlemen (further on, it is life itself: the future survivors of the slaughter wear a green ribbon); and since two sites of the female body can be deflowered, front and back, the mark is a dual one, of appropriation (to a certain libertine) and of localization:

Gentlemen	Front	Behind
Duc de Blangis	pink	green
The Bishop	0	violet
Durcet	0	lilac
Curval	black	yellow

(The Bishop and Durcet provide themselves with no "fronts" for defloration: the degree zero of defloration, a signifying status if there ever was one, since it proclaims these two Gentlemen to be pure sodomites). In this table, it is the very being of the mark, of any mark, that is revealed: it is at once an indication of ownership (like the brand on cattle), an act of identification (like a soldier's serial number) and a fetishist gesture, cutting up the body, promoting and contrasting two of its parts. All these aims are to be found in the linguistic nature of the mark: as we know, it is the basic act of meaning; and Sade is actually constructing before our eyes a twofold paradigm: on one side colors, on the other the Gentlemen and the sites. Ownership, merchandise, and fetish come together in the meaning.

The Helmet

The scream is the victim's mark: she makes herself a victim because she chooses to scream; if, under the same vexation, she were to ejaculate, she would cease to be a victim, would be transformed into a libertine: *to scream/to discharge,* this paradigm is the beginning of choice, i.e., Sadian meaning. The best proof is that if a sentence begins with the narrative of a vexation, it is impossible to know who is speaking, since it is impossible to predict whether it will end in screams or in ejaculation: the sentence is free up until the last moment: "Verneuil then pinched her buttocks with a strength so cruel . . ." (we expect something like: "that the victim was unable to restrain her screams"; however, what we get from the syntactical machine, from the posture-sentence, is quite the opposite): ". . . that the whore came on the spot." (Similarly, inversely: " 'My child,' said the Marquis, whom one night spent with Justine . . . had surprisingly set against that girl.")

Yet this scream which distinguishes the victim is also, contradictorily, nothing but the attribute, the accessory, the amorous supplement, bombast. Whence the value of a machine to isolate the scream and deliver it to the libertine as a delightful part of the victim's body, i.e., as a sonorous fetish: this is the tubed helmet that is rigged up on Mme de Verneuil's head; it is "arranged so that the screams drawn from her by the pain inflicted on her resembled the lowing of a cow." This singular bonnet has a threefold advantage: since the victim is shut up with her torturer in a solitary, the helmet transmits her pain to the other libertines outside as if by radio, without their seeing the scene: supreme pleasure, they can imagine it, i.e., fantasize it; further, without taking away any of its descriptive power, the helmet denatures the scream, stamps it with an animal foreignness, transforming the "pale, melancholy and distinguished woman" into a bovine mass; lastly, the tube, vagina or colon, injects a sonorous rod into the libertine, a musical turd (the turd is precisely excrement reduced to phallic state): the scream is a fetish.

The Division of Languages

In his *Notes littéraires,* Sade reports without comment Marie Antoinette's words in the Conciergerie: "The ferocious beasts surrounding me each day invent some new humiliation to add to the horror of my fate; they are distilled day by day," etc. It has been thought (Lély) that Sade copied these words because he was applying them to himself. I read the quotation otherwise: as an example of victimal language: Antoinette and Justine speak the same language, the same style. Sade does not comment upon the fallen queen's situation, he does not define the victim by the practice in which she is caught up ("to suffer," "to endure," "to receive"); an exorbitant thing, if we recall the common definition of sadism and the structural definition of character, here the "role" is considered negligible. The victim is not *he or she who submits,* but *he or she who uses a certain language.* In the Sadian novel—as in the Proustian—the population is divided into classes not according to practice, but according to language, or more precisely, according to the practice of language (undissociable from any real practice): Sadian characters are *language actors*. (If we wanted completely to extend this notion to the very genre of the novel, we would have to elaborate a whole new narrative grammar: against the epic or the tale, isn't the novel the new narrative in which the division of labor—of classes—is crowned with a division of languages?)

Confession

The function of confession, a religious rite Sade greatly enjoys putting into his orgies, is not only ignominiously to parody the sacrament of penitence or to illustrate the sadistic situation of the subject submitting to her executioner; into the "scene" (erotic, combative, and theatrical episode), it introduces a duplicity not only of meaning, but of space. As in the medieval spectacle, two sites are presented for reading *at the same time,* either the libertine simultaneously hears and sees what theology separates, i.e., Soul and Body ("He wanted his daughter to confess to a monk he had won over . . . thus he can hear his daughter's confession and see her ass at the same time"), or the reader, set before the confessional as before a split stage, contemplates at a glance, in one compartment, Justine kneeling, her eyes toward heaven, making a candid confession, and in another the monk Severino hearing Justine with a half-naked fuckee between his legs. A complex and paradoxical aesthetic object is thereby produced: sound and sight are linked in the spectacle (which is banal) but separated by the bar of the confessional, by the classifying Law (*soul/body*) at the basis of transgression: the stereography is complete.

Dissertation, Scene

Anyone leafing through Sade's books knows that they alternate two principal kinds of typography: closely printed, uninterrupted pages: the over-all philosophical dissertation;

pages with blank spaces, indentations, ellipses, exclamation marks, a taut, interrupted, staggered language: the orgy, the libidinous or criminal scene. Whatever the reading habit (more or less lazy), these two blocks are equal: the dissertation is an erotic object.

It is not only speech that is erogenous, not only what it represents (by definition, the dissertation paints nothing whatever, but the libertine, infinitely more aware than the Sadian reader, is excited by it, not bored), it is the subtlest, most cultivated forms of the discourse: *reasoning* (" 'What?' Nicolette said, 'you don't want me to miss my fucking, when my father reasons so well?' "), *system* (" 'Sir, are you getting hard?' . . . 'It's true . . . these systems aroused my imagination' "), *maxim* ("Coeur de Fer aroused himself by exposing these wise maxims"). Juliette thus naturally ranks the dissertation among the extravagant pleasures she demands from Pope Braschi in return for the ardor she promises him; she names it, pell-mell, along with theft, the black mass, the lavish orgy.

The dissertation "seduces," "animates," "misleads," "electrifies," "inflames"; in the series of orgies, it indubitably functions as a rest period, but this rest is not merely for ordinary recuperation: during the dissertation, erotic energy is renewed. The libertine body, *of which language is a part,* is a homeostatic apparatus that maintains itself: the scene requires justification, discourse; this discourse inflames, eroticizes; the libertine "cannot hold out"; a new scene begins, and so on, *ad infinitum.*

The Language Space

The principal site at the Château de Silling is the theater of debauchery where everyone meets daily from 5 to 10 P.M. In this theater, everyone is actor and spectator. The area is therefore simultaneously that of a *mimesis,* here purely auditory, consigned to the storyteller's narrative, and

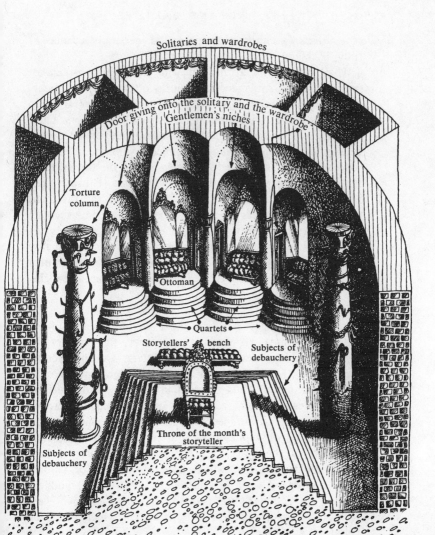

Solitaries and wardrobes

Door giving onto the solitary and the wardrobe

Gentlemen's niches

Torture
column

Ottoman

Quartets

Storytellers' bench

Subjects of
debauchery

Throne of the month's
storyteller

Subjects of
debauchery

of a *praxis* (a conjunction attempted, generally unsuccessfully, by many avant-garde theaters).

Here Speech is enthroned, the prestigious organ of *mimesis.* The Gentlemen, each on his ottoman, in his niche, at his feet his quartet of subjects who form an integral group (in every sense) with him, are at first only Auditors. On a bench, the three storytellers who are off duty make up the reserve of speech, just as the subjects who are not being used in the appropriate foursomes, sitting on the steps of the proscenium, make up the reserve of vice. Thus between Mimesis and Praxis (which will be sited on the ottomans and in the chambers on the mezzanine), an intermediate space, that of virtuality, extends: the discourse traverses this space, and in this traversal it is gradually transformed into practices: the story being told becomes the program for an action whose subsidiary theater is the ottoman, the niche, the solitary.

The total space is—diagrammatically—that of language. Around the throne, issued by the Founding Speech of the Storyteller, Language, Code, Competence, the units of the combinative, the elements of the System. On the Gentlemen's side, Minted Speech, Performance, Syntagm, the Spoken Sentence. Thus the Sadian theater (and precisely because it is a theater) is not that ordinary place where we prosaically pass from speech to fact (in line with the empirical design of *application*), but the stage of the primal text, that of the Storyteller (herself the product of how many anterior codes), which traverses a transformational space and engenders a second text, whose primary auditors become its secondary utterers: an unending movement (are we not in turn the readers of both texts?) which is the attribute of writing.

Irony

It appears that the separation of languages is respected in every society, as though each one were a chemical substance and could not come into contact with a supposedly contrary language without producing a social conflagration. Sade spends his time producing these explosive metonymies. The sentence, simultaneously, as a form, *sufficient and brief,* serves as his combustion chamber. The high, pompous, cultural styles coded by centuries of orthodox literature are summoned to appear in this little theater of the sentence side by side with the pornogram: *maxim* (Female recluses: "they are not linked by virtue, but by fucking"), *lyric apostrophe* ("Fuck, O my companions, you were born to fuck"), *praise of virtue* ("I owe to his firm character the justice of saying that he did not come once"), *poetic metaphor* ("Obliged to relieve a member he could no longer keep in his pants, he let it spring out into the air and presented to us the image of a young shrub cut loose from its bonds, bending for an instant its summit toward the earth").

We note: Sade suppresses the aesthetic division of languages; however, Sade does not suppress in line with a naturalistic model, (illusorily) allowing the direct, so-called uncultural (or popular) language to break through the surface: culture cannot be overthrown by a verbal coup: it can only be *ruined*—leave on the new field of language a few moments despoiled of their context and their superb past, and yet still possessing the highly elaborate grace, the delicious patina, the necessary distance which centuries of rhetorical courtesy have given them. This method of destruction (by the ill-timed citation of token throwbacks) constitutes Sade's *irony.*

The Voyage

No one ever calls Sade a picaresque novelist (one of the rare ones in our French literature). The apparent reason for this "oversight" is that the Sadian adventurer (Juliette, Justine) is always traversing one sole adventure, and this adventure is vulgar.

Yet the most vulgar of censures (of morals) always conceals some ideological profit: if the Sadian novel is excluded from our literature, it is because in it novelistic peregrination is never a quest for the Unique (temporal essence, truth, happiness), but a repetition of pleasure; Sadian errancy is *unseemly,* not because it is vicious and criminal, but because it is dull and somehow insignificant, withdrawn from transcendency, void of term: it does not reveal, does not transform, does not develop, does not educate, does not sublimate, does not accomplish, recuperates nothing, save for the present itself, cut up, glittering, repeated; no patience, no experience; everything is carried immediately to the acme of knowledge, of power, of ejaculation; time does not arrange or derange it, it repeats, recalls, recommences, there is no scansion other than that which alternates the formation and the expenditure of sperm.

There is also in the Sadian voyage a seeming disrespect for the "vocation" of the novel itself. *Juliette* and *Justine,* its reverse, are to the novelistic quest what cruising is to real love: what are all these picaresque heroes and heroines, Juliette, Jérôme, Brisa-Testa, Clairwil, and even Justine, doing, but cruising? They cruise for partners, victims, accomplices, torturers, "chicken." Yet, just as amorous pursuit, far from obnubilating the cruiser, keeps him continuously aware of the world around him and gives him a finer sensibility, a curiosity more aware of the total area through which he moves (the cruiser—if one wishes, Don Juan— travels in a basically more disinterested way than the tourist, swaddled in the stereotypes of monuments, since for him the culture comes under the *indirect*), so the Sadian pursuit causes to pass before our eyes—without *appropriating* it under the guise of truth—an entire historical Europe: social classes, financial practices, eating habits, clothes, furnishings, transportation, up to and including great figures of this monarchical society (the King of Naples, the Cardinal de Bernis, Frederick II, Henri, Sophie of Prussia,

Victor Amédée of Sardinia, Catherine II, Pius VI), whose
derisory figuration in no way extenuates the historical sign
they constitute, toward and against all the unreal debaucheries in which they participate.

Sade the Precursor

Debauchery is imaginative; under its impulsion, Sade invented: radio transmission (the scream helmet enables the
libertines to live, without seeing them, the tortures carried
out in the next room: the mere sonorous information causes
them to ejaculate, as it enables the modern auditor to
dramatize) and the cinema (at Cardoville's, on the outskirts
of Lyons, Dolmus imagines a "divine scene": every part of
Justine's body, put up for lottery, will be molested by a
libertine: "each one in turn will naughtily make the patient
suffer the pain assigned him. These turns will be rapidly
alternated; we will imitate the ticking of a clock": an as-
tonishing disposition, for in the Sadian film, no one—no *I*—
is actually the subject of the sequence: no one is filming it,
no one is projecting it, no one is seeing it: a continuous
image is locked on nothing but time, the clock).

Libertine Poetics

What is a paradigm? an opposition of terms that cannot
be simultaneously realized. The paradigm is very moral: a
time for everything, do not confuse, etc., and thereby meaning, the dispenser of law, clarity, security, will be founded.
In Sade, the victim desires law, wants meaning, respects the
paradigm; the libertine, on the other hand, strives to broaden,
i.e., destroy them: since language proposes a separation of
transgressions (*incest/parricide*), the libertine will do anything to join the terms (to be both incestuous and a parricide, and especially to force someone else to commit the
same transgression), the victim will do anything to resist

this jumbling together and to maintain the incommunication between the criminal morphemes (Cloris, Saint-Fond's victim, on whom he works his will, "is incestuous in order not to become a parricide").

Machines

Sade often invents real machines, sensual or criminal. There are apparatuses for producing suffering: a fustigator (it dilates the flesh to allow the blood to flow quickly), a raper (at Minski's), an impregnator (i.e., to prepare for infanticide), a laugh maker (producing "so violent a pain that it produces a sardonic laugh extremely strange to experience"). There are machines to produce ejaculation: the most elaborate belongs to the Prince of Francaville, the richest lord of Naples: a woman getting into it receives a soft, flexible dildo which, worked on a spring, subjects her to a perpetual friction; every fifteen minutes, "jets of a hot, sticky liquid, whose odor and viscosity made it easily mistakable for the purest and freshest sperm," are released into her vagina, while from another source the machine, having become a fetishist, isolates the parts to be caressed and ceaselessly refreshes them; finally, there are machines that combine both functions, being cruelly threatening in order to force one into the proper posture.

The Sadian machine does not stop at the automaton (the century's craze); the whole group of the living is conceived, constructed like a machine. In its canonical state (Justine admitted to the Convent of Sainte-Marie-des-Bois, for example), it includes a substructure constructed around the basic patient (here Justine) and saturated when all the body's sites are occupied by different partners ("Let's all six of us get on top of her"); from this basic architecture, defined by rule of catalysis, an open apparatus extends whose sites increase whenever a partner is added to the initial group; the machine will tolerate no one's being solitary, no one's remaining outside it: Gernande indicates to Dorothée, who has remained off to one side, how to enter into the group ("Slip in under my wife"); the machine *in toto* is a well-balanced system ("Justine supports them all, the entire weight is upon her alone") and open: what defines it is the interlocking of all the parts ("The two operations dovetail, harmonize together") which interconnect as though they knew their role by heart and without any improvisation being necessary ("All the women instantly form six ranks"). Once set up, the living machine has but to start up, to "go" ("Let us now work together"). Once in operation, it shakes and makes a bit of noise, owing to the convulsive movements of the participants ("Nothing is so libidinous to see as the convulsive movements of this group made up of twenty-one persons"). There remains but to look after it, like a good overseer who paces along, lubricating, tightening, regulating, changing, etc. ("Marthe walks along the ranks; she wipes off the balls, sees to it that . . ." etc.).

Colors

The colors of clothing are signs. On one hand, classes of age and functions (catamites, jockeys, agents, fuckers, virgins, well-bred girls, duennas, etc.), on the other, colors. The relationship between the two correlates is mutually arbitrary (unmotivated). However, as in language, a certain analogy is set up, a proportional rapport, a diagrammatic relationship: the color increases in intensity, brilliance, fire, as the age increases and sensual pleasure ripens: the young catamites (7 to 12 years of age) are in gray, as though this pale gray signified the insipidity, the passivity natural to their age; older (12 to 18), they become purple and then, having become agents (19 to 25), they are dressed in bronze-colored dress coats; at Gernande's, the great libertines have scarlet collars, their heads adorned with flaming red turbans.

Scene, Machine, Writing

"What a lovely group!" La Durande exclaims, seeing Juliette "occupied" by four thieves from Ancona. The Sadian group is often a pictorial or sculptural object: the discourse captures the figures of debauchery not only as arranged, architectured, but above all as frozen, framed, lighted; it treats them as *tableaux vivants*. This form of theater has been little studied, doubtless because no one does it any more. However, must we be reminded that for a long time the *tableau vivant* was a bourgeois entertainment, analogous to the charade? as a child, the present author on several occasions attended, at pious and provincial charity bazaars, performances of grand *tableaux vivants*—Sleeping Beauty, for example; he did not know that this social game is of the same fantasmatic essence as the Sadian tableau; perhaps he came to understand that later by observing that the filmic photogram is opposed to film itself because of a split which is not created by its having been extracted (one immobilizes and publishes a scene taken from a great film), but, one might say, by its having been perverted: the *tableau vivant,* despite the apparently total character of the figuration, is a fetish object (to immobilize, to light, to frame, means to *cut up*), whereas film, as *function,* is an hysterical activity (the cinema does not consist in animating images; the opposition between photography and film is not that of the fixed and the mobile image; cinema consists not in figuring, but in a system's *being made to function*).

Now, despite the predominance of *tableaux,* this split exists in the Sadian text and, it appears, for the same purposes. For the "group" which is in fact a photogram of debauchery, is contrasted here and there with a *moving scene.* The vocabulary charged with denoting this commotion within the group (which virtually changes its nature, philosophically) is an extensive one (*to execute, to continue, to vary, to break up, to disarrange*). We know that this *functioning* scene is nothing but a machine without subject, since there is even an automatic ticking ("Minski approaches the hitched-up creature and fondles his buttocks, bites them, and all the women *instantly* form six ranks"). Before the *tableau vivant*—and the *tableau vivant* is precisely that *before* which I place myself—there is by definition, by the finality of the genre, a Spectator, a fetishist, a pervert (Sade, the narrator, a character, the reader, no matter). On the other hand, in the moving scene, this subject, leaving his armchair, his gallery, his orchestra seat, crosses the footlights, enters into the screen, incorporates himself into the time, the variations, and the breaks in the act of vice, in short, into its game: there is passage from representation to labor. (In Sade, there is a mixed genre, a *tableau vivant* for the reader, a scene for the partners: thus the vast baroque syntagm which shows us, in a very Fellinian sequence, Noirceuil and his acolytes, in sub-zero weather, dressed in enormous furs, making naked young Fontange jump about on a frozen pond by bombarding her and lashing at her with their long whips.)

A transitory historical site, Sadian writing contains this twofold postulate. Either it represents the *tableau vivant,* respects the identity of painting and classical writing, which holds that one need only *describe* what has already been painted and what it calls "reality"; it cites this *already* composed referent in giving itself architecture (*left/right*), color, relationships, nuances, light, touch. Or it leaves representation: unable to figure (eternalize) what moves, varies, breaks up, it loses the power of description and can only *allege* functioning, give its generic total: to say *that works* is not to write, but to relate. Hence we see the ambiguity of classical writing: figurative, it can only present objects, essences, spatially situated, the object of the (pictorial, literary) art then being, relentlessly, the renewal of the objects' relationship, i.e., *composition;* in short, it cannot describe labor; in order to become "modern," it has to invent a language activity completely other than description and pass, as Mallarmé hoped it would, from the *tableau vivant* to the "scene" (to scenography).

In the past, there existed—variations of the music boxes which were a Swiss specialty—"mechanical pictures": classical paintings, in which, however, some element was made to move mechanically: the hands of the village clock moved, or the farmer's wife moved her legs, or the cow raised its head to low. This somewhat archaic status is that of the Sadian scene: it is a *tableau vivant* in which something begins to move; movement is added sporadically, the spectator joins in, not by projection but by intrusion; and this mixture of figure and labor then becomes very modern: the theater has tried very hard to bring the actors into the audience, but this procedure is ridiculous; rather, the inverse movement should be imagined: some vast erotic *tableau,* conceived, composed, framed, lit, where the most libidinous figures would be represented through the very materiality of bodies, and instead of the actors jumping into the auditorium vulgarly to provoke the spectator, the spectator would go onto the stage and *join in* the posture: "What a lovely group!" says La Durand, thereby founding the *tableau vivant* ("Juliette and the Thieves"), but transforming the *tableau* into a production, she goes on to say: "Come, my friend . . . let's join in the *tableau,* let's form one of its episodes"; the ensemble, scene and *tableau,* will be *written*—and will even be pure writing: an image open to the eruption of a labor: because at the moment when figuration disappears, labor begins to register (this is the whole adventure of non-figurative painting, and of the Text).

Language and Crime

Let us (if we can) imagine a society without language. Here is a man copulating with a woman, *a tergo,* and using in the act a bit of wheat paste. On this level, no perversion. Only by the progressive addition of some nouns does the crime gradually *develop,* grow in volume, in consistency, and attain the highest degree of transgression. The man is called the *father* of the woman he is possessing, who is described as being *married;* the amorous act is ignominiously termed *sodomy;* and the bit of bread bizarrely associated in this act becomes, under the noun *host,* a religious symbol whose flouting is sacrilege. Sade excels in *collecting* this pile of language: for him, the sentence has this function of founding crime: the syntax, refined by centuries of culture, becomes an *elegant* (in the sense we use the word in mathematics, a solution is elegant) art; it collects crime with exactitude and address: "To unite incest, adultery, sodomy, and sacrilege, he buggers his married daughter with a host."

Homonymy

In Sadian *art de vivre* it is not so much a question of multiplying pleasures, of making them revolve, creating out of them a dizzying carrousel (this rapid succession will terminate the Party), as of superposing them (this simultaneity would define what we might call sybaritism). Thus, "Killing a pregnant woman": "There are two pleasures in one: what we call *cow and calf.*" The addition of pleasures provides a supplementary pleasure, that of the addition itself; in Sadian arithmetic, the total becomes in turn a unit which is added to its components: " 'And do you not see that what you are daring to do simultaneously bears the imprint of two or three crimes . . . ?' 'Well, really, madame, precisely what you have just told me is going to make me come even more pleasurably.' " This superior pleasure, completely formal, since it is in sum only a mathematical notion, is a language pleasure: that of unfolding a criminal act into different nouns: "I am thus simultaneously committing incest, adultery, sodomy": it is homonymy that is voluptuous.

Striptease

In Sade, no striptease. The body is uncovered at once (save for a few young men who are allowed to "let their pants fall agreeably down over their thighs"). Here, perhaps, is the reason. The striptease is a narrative: it develops in time the terms ("classemes") of a code which is that of the Enigma: from the outset, the unveiling of a secret is promised, then withheld ("suspended"), and finally both accomplished and avoided; like narrative, the striptease is subject to a logico-temporal order, a constraint of the code that constitutes it (the first being not to uncover the sexual organ). Now, in Sade there is no bodily secret to seek, but only a practice to achieve; invention, emotion, surprise, do not spring from a secret that is postulated and then violated, but from the flowerings of a combinative sought in the open, through an order that is not logical, but merely serial: the sexual (or counter-sexual) organ in Sade is not a center, the belated and time-honored object of a *final* manifestation (of an epiphany); the adventure begins further along: when the body, immediately denuded, offers all its sites to be molested or occupied. As narrative, the striptease has the same function as Revelation, it is a part of Occidental hermeneutics. Sade is materialistic in that he substitutes practical language for secret language: the scene is terminated not by the unveiling of the truth (sexual organ) but by ejaculation.

The Pornogram

Sade makes pornograms. The pornogram is not merely the written trace of an erotic practice, nor even the product of a cutting up of that practice, treated as a grammar of sites and operations; through a new chemistry of the text, it is the fusion (as under high temperature) of discourse and body. ("You see me completely naked," Eugénie says to her professor: "dissertate on me as much as you want"), so that, that point having been reached, the writing will be what regulates the exchange of Logos and Eros, and that it will be possible to speak of the erotic as a grammarian and of language as a pornographer.

The Language of Augustin

Augustin is the young gardener, delightfully well built, around eighteen years of age, whom the libertines of *The Boudoir* take on as a mannequin for their teaching and as a subject of their pleasures.

His social standing is marked twice: first by the peasant style of his speech ("Gollee, what a purty mouth. . . . It's so fresh . . . I might have my nose stuck in the roses in our garden. . . . And, sir, you can see how that pleasures me!"), a style that the aristocratic society somewhat snobbishly enjoys as rural exoticism ("Ah, charming . . . charming!"); next, and more seriously, by the exclusion from language that is imposed upon him: when Dolmancé is preparing to read his companions the pamphlet "Frenchmen, a bit more effort if you want to be republicans," Augustin is sent out: "Go away, Augustin, this is not for you; but don't go far; we will ring when you are to return." Which means: (1) morality is reversed: where ordinarily one makes a child leave in order not to hear an adult's obscenities, Sade makes the subject leave the debauchery so that he will not hear the libertines' serious discourse: a kind of black frame set around the screen of the text; (2) the discourse that founds a republican morality is, paradoxically, an act of linguistic secession; the popular tongue, at first amusingly contrasted with aristocratic language, is then simply excluded from the Dissertation, i.e., the ex-

change (between Logos and Eros); the libidinous scene is
an unrestricted mixture of bodies but not of languages:
panic eroticism stops all the division of sociolectics; Augustin represents that ultimate limit in an exemplary way, insofar as he is not a victim (no harm will come to him): he is
the pure *common man* who gives the freshness of his body
and his speech: he is not humiliated, simply excluded.

The Complaisance of the Sentence

Concerning Christ's mother's virginity, the Middle Ages
were most amazed by the subversion of grammar: that the
Creator made Himself man, that a virgin should conceive,
led in sum (but is it not *the ultimate delving into the question?*) to an inversion of voices (passive becoming active),
to an upsetting of semantic classes: it was an alliance of
words that stupefied, the stoppage of every grammatical
rule (*in hac verbi copula stupet omnis regula*). Sade, too,
knows that the perfection of a perverse pose is indissociable
from the phrastic model whereby it is uttered. Rhetorical
symmetry, elegant foreshortening, exact balance, the solidarity of active and passive, the entire art of discourse, in
short, diagrammatically figures the art of sensual pleasure:
"She obtains from this lovely girl's fingers the same services
her tongue renders to me": extended by the most elegant
of figures, chiasmus (*obtain . . . / . . . render*), the paradigm
becomes the condition of pleasure, which cannot exist outside this total complaisance of the sentence, without this
intelligence, both mental and complicit, of syntax.

Bringing Order

"Considering that it is much more preferable for pleasure
that things occur in an orderly manner . . ." This is not
Sade speaking, it is Brahms (in a notice to the women of the
Hamburg Choir); but it could be Sade (" 'Friends,' said the

monk, 'let's put some order into these proceedings' "; or:
" 'One moment,' she said, enflamed, 'an instant, my dear
friends, let's put a bit of order into our pleasures, we will
not ejaculate unless we fix them,' " etc.).

Order is necessary for vice, i.e., transgression; order is
precisely that which separates transgression from conten-
tion. This is because vice is an area of exchange: one practice for one pleasure; "excesses" must be profitable; thus
they must be subject to an economy, and this economy must
be planned. Nevertheless, the Sadian planner is neither
tyrant nor proprietor nor technocrat: he has no permanent
hold over his partners' bodies, he has no special jurisdic-
tion; he is a very temporary master of ceremonies who will
not fail to join the scene he has just programmed as quickly
as he can: from it, he derives no sensual pleasure superior
to that of his companions; of the pleasure he has just organized with his words, he retains nothing *more* for himself;
he launches the pleasure merchandise, but it circulates without ever insisting on a surplus value (ejaculation or prestige); his function is somewhat analogous (whence the encounter with innocent Brahms) to that of an orchestra conductor who leads his colleagues from his violin desk (by
playing himself) without being set apart from the others.
The person regulating pleasure is ordinarily a human subject; however, the libertines can readily decide, on occasion,
that it will be luck: the game of postures is decided by a
lottery that attaches a certain number to a certain part of
the victim's body, and each draws the number of his
pleasure: chance thus appears as a de-alienating order; the
structure of pleasures, essential to their operation, can no
longer be suspected of owing anything to any Law, any subject: all of rhetoric, and in sum, all of politics, is overthrown
without the group's ceasing to receive its pleasure from this
operation whose origin, reversing itself, is lost in the very
game it has produced.

Exchange

We really think that Narrative (as an anthropological practice) is based on some exchange: a narrative is offered,
received, structured *for* (or *against*) some thing, of which
it is somehow the *ponderable*. But what? Of course, we can
see that in Balzac's *Sarrasine* the narrative is exchanged
against a night of love, and that in *The Thousand and One
Nights* each new story is worth a day of life to Schehera-
zade; however, this is because then the exchange is represented in the narrative itself: the narrative recounts the contract of which it is the object. This happens twice in Sade.
First, throughout his work, the author, the characters, and
the readers exchange a dissertation for a scene: philosophy
is the price (i.e., the meaning) of vice (or reciprocally).
And then, in *The 120 Days,* the narrative (as in *The
Thousand and One Nights*) is equivalent to life itself: the
first Storyteller, whose function, established by the libertines, is precisely to raise the Story (Narrative) like a
sacred object over the assembly (she speaks from a throne),
to expose it like a luxury merchandise of enormous price
(wasn't this mad voyage to Silling, so similar in structure
to the initiation voyages of popular tales, organized to
gather the Herb of Life, the Gold of Superpower, the talis-
man, the Treasure of Speech?). La Duclos, in fact, in exchange for the great coprophagic Narrative (articulated in
150 anecdotes) which she delivers sumptuously ("in very
thin and very elegant deshabille, much rouge and many dia-
monds"), obtains from the Gentlemen the promise that "to
no matter what extent they may be turned against women
during the voyage, she will always be well treated and very
certainly brought back home to Paris." Nothing says this
solemn contract is going to be honored: what is a libertine's
promise *worth,* other than the pleasure of cheating on it? The
exchange thus leaks away: the contract underlying the nar-

rative is stated so strongly only that it may be more surely broken: the future of the sign is the betrayal in which it will be taken. Still, this defection is possible and desirable only because one has solemnly pretended to establish the exchange, the sign, the meaning.

The Dictation

How can pleasure be *invented?* Here is the technique Juliette recommends to the beautiful Countess de Donis:

1. *Ascesis:* forgo libertine notions for two weeks (if need be by amusing oneself with other things).

2. *Disposition:* go to bed alone, in peace, silence, and total darkness and indulge in a bit of self-abuse.

3. *Release:* all images, all distractions set aside during the period of ascesis are set free in disorder, without exception: they are given an over-all review: "The world is yours."

4. *Choice:* among the *tableaux* that pass before you, one asserts itself and gives rise to ejaculation.

5. *Sketching:* the candles must be relit and the scene transcribed in a notebook (tablets).

6. *Correction:* after having slept and allowed this first sketch to rest, one begins to fantasize the argument jotted down, adding anything that can revive the image, grown a bit tired owing to the ejaculation it has already provided.

7. *Text:* form a written corpus of the image hereby remembered and augmented. The next step is to "commit" this image, this crime, this passion.

The scene of vice is thus preceded and formed by a scene of writing. Everything occurs at the dictation of fantasy: it is guided. The real (or so-called real, since in the end it is only described—we should be able to say: de-scribed—by Sade) scene is nothing but a *poem,* the product of a poetic technique, such as Horace or Quintilian might have conceived. In it we find the principal moments of classical labor:

isolate oneself, prepare oneself, imagine (allow the Muse to come), choose, write, let rest, correct; the difference is that in Sadian writing correction is never crossing out, it is not castrative, but only augmentative: a paradoxical technique practiced by few writers, among whom, however, are Rousseau, Stendhal, Balzac, and Proust. This fantasy dictation is to be found in Ignatius Loyola, whose *Spiritual Exercises* is marked by the same protocols (retreat, darkness, imagination, repetition).

The fantasy is a *dictator* (the one whose profession it was, in the Middle Ages, to dictate letters and rule the art of *dictamen,* an important variety of rhetorical genre): everything comes into play in this *dictation.* The dictation written by Juliette opens up a reversion of texts: the image appears to originate a program, the program a text, and the text a practice; however, this practice is itself written, it returns (for the reader) to program, to text, to fantasy: nothing remains but an inscription with a multiple tense: fantasy *announces* memory, writing is not anamnesis but catamnesis. And this is the ambiguous meaning of any dictation: this stupid exercise, caught in an ideological matrix (since it has the function of ensuring the mastery of orthography, a class act, if there ever was one), this barren childhood memory is also the powerful trace of an anterior text that is *taken,* thereby reintroducing the fragments of a language into our daily life and opening reality to the infinity of texts: what is "spring," the one we actually await with such impatience (and most usually disappointment) around mid-April, when we conceive a longing for the countryside, begin to buy new clothes, but Jean Aicard's "Spring," which was dictated to us one day in school? The origin of spring is not the elliptical revolution of our globe, it is a dictation, i.e., a false origin. When the monk Sylvestre forces Aurore and Justine to insult him and molest him while he prepares to sacrifice his daughter, he makes them write down *in advance* in blasphemies and reproaches the murder he is going to commit: Aurore and Justine "draw their text from the crime the scoundrel will commit": Sylvestre, *scriptor emeritus,* is well aware that the tense of the writing *turns* (like a spiral).

The Chain

The Sadian relationship (between two libertines) is not one of reciprocity but of revenge (Lacan): revenge is a simple *turn,* a combinative movement: "Now a temporary victim, my angel, and soon a persecutor . . ." This gliding (from recognition to mere availability) ensures the immorality of human relationships (libertines are complaisant, but they also kill one another): the line is not dual, but plural; not only are friendships (if they occur) revocable, they circulate (Juliette, Olympe, Clairwil, La Durand), but above all, any erotic conjunction tends to depart from the monogamous formula: for the *couple,* whenever possible, is substituted the *chain* (which the Bolognese nuns practice under the name *rosary*). The meaning of the chain is to posit the infinity of erotic language (isn't the sentence itself a chain?), to break the mirror of the utterance, to act so that pleasure does not return to its point of departure, to squander the exchange by dissociating the partners, not to give back to whoever gives to you, to give to whoever will not give back, to send the cause, the origin, *elsewhere,* to make one person terminate the gesture begun by another: every chain is open, its saturation is only provisional: it produces nothing internal, nothing *interior.*

Grammar

If I say there is a Sadian erotic grammar (a porno-grammar)—with its erotemes and combining rules—that does not mean I have a hold over the Sadian text in the manner of a grammarian (in fact, who will denounce our linguists' image reservoir?). I merely mean that to Sade's ritual (struc-

tured by Sade himself under the name *scene*) must respond
(but not correspond) another pleasure ritual, which is the
labor of reading, reading at work: there is labor as soon as
the relationship between the two texts is not a mere *compte-
rendu;* my hand is not guided by truth, but by the game, the
truth of the game. It has been said that there is no meta-
language: or rather, there are only meta-languages, *language upon language,* like a foliation without a kernel, or
better yet, because no language has control over another,
the game of topping hands.

Silence

Aside from the screams of the victims, aside from blas-
phemings, both of which form part of the ritual's efficacy, a
profound silence is imposed at every scene of vice. In the
great rout organized by the Société des Amis du Crime, "one
could have heard a fly buzz." This silence is the silence of the
libidinous machine, so well oiled, brought to such easy
efficiency that we can distinguish only a few sighs, quiver-
ings; especially, however, like the sovereign reserve of the
great ascetic practices (such as Zen), the creation of a dis-
infected sonorous space attests to bodily control, the mastery
of figures, order of the scene; it is, in a word, an heroic,
aristocratic value, a *virtue:* "The votaries assembled by
Venus did not wish to disturb their mysteries with any of
those disgusting vociferations that are appropriate only to
pedantism and imbecility": it is in order *not to resemble* the
erotic "shows" of the petit bourgeoisie that the Sadian orgy
is silent.

The Bottom of the Page

Saint-Florent, one of Justine's persecutors, is thereby,
justly, an adorable libertine, in line with the exalted descriptions Sade gives of the heroes of Evil. Yet, by confiding to
us in a footnote that Saint-Florent actually lived, in Lyons,
Sade, highly indignant, adds that he was an execrable mon-

ster. Similarly, the list of crimes, debaucheries, ignominies
of the popes serves to discredit religion, but that same list,
read in context, we might say, is that of the great libertines
Sade admires. These two instances, that of the "real" and
that of the discourse, never meet: no dialectic joins them,
gives them a common, articulated meaning, and therefore,
in Saint-Florent's case, the "real" is uttered *on another part
of the page,* in a footnote which incorporates the loss (in
the case of the popes, the list is typographically separated
from the story like an incongruous supplement, an appen-
dix). The Text is this cutting; the Text is not unrealistic,
it does not modestly ignore the referent that might impede
its falsehood; it cuts, but it does not strike out; it achieves
itself in logical defiance, in heated contradiction.

Ritual

Law, no. Protocol, yes. The most libertarian of writers
wants Ceremony, Party, Rite, Discourse. In the Sadian
scene there is someone "commanding the discharges, pre-
scribing substitutions, and presiding over the whole order
of the orgies"; there is someone (but no more than "someone") who makes up the program, traces the perspective
(ordinator and orderer). This is the opposite of the dull
"partouze" where everyone wants to keep his "freedom,"
immediatize his desires. The rite, from *elsewhere,* but no
person, is here imposed upon ejaculation. It appears that
this is what separates the Sadian text from other transgressions (the drug trip, for example). As a combinative,
Sadian eroticism is neither sensual nor mystical. The diffrac-
tion of the subject is substituted for his dissolution.

Proper Nouns

The robustness of French common names: Foucolet
(masochistic president of the Chambre des Comptes),
Gareau, Ribert, Vernol, Maugin (beggars), Latour (a
valet), Marianne Lavergne, Mariette Borelly, Mariannette

Laugier, Rose Coste, Jeanne Nicou (Marseilles prostitutes).

The rectitude of surnames: Brise-Cul [Ass breaker] (he has a crooked cock), Bande-au-Ciel [Sky-high erection], Clairwil (the clear will of the most inflexible of the libertines is uttered by the sharpest of vowels: her name has the same significance as her diet: white chicken meat, iced water with lemon and orange).

The beauty of natural names: Sade's genealogy: Bertrande de Bagnols, Emessende de Salves, Rostain de Morières, Bernard d'Ancezune, Verdaine de Trentelivres, Barthelémy d'Oppède, Sibille de Jarente, Diane de Simiane; Hugues, Raimonde, Augière, Guillaumette, Audrivet, Aigline—soldiers at the fort of Miolans where Sade was imprisoned: Violence, Happiness.

An extreme, loving, delicate, and rightful attention to the sovereign signifier: the proper noun. In his notes, Sade writes: "Ziza, a pretty name to use," "Alaire, a pretty name to write down," "Maseline, pretty name for a man."

Thievery, Prostitution

To steal from the rich, force the poor to prostitute themselves, are rational, empirical, banal operations; they can in no way constitute transgressions. Transgression is created by the reversal of violations; crime begins only in form, and paradox is the purest of forms: thus we must steal from the poor and prostitute the rich; Verneuil will only agree to sodomize Dorothée d'Esterval if she demands a great deal of money from him: "They say you are rich, madame? Well, in that case I must pay you: were you poor, I would rob you."

Sewing

Among the tortures Sade imagines (a monotonous, scarcely terrifying list, since it is most often based on the butcher shop, i.e., on abstraction), only one is disturbing: that which consists in sewing the victim's anus or vagina (in

The Boudoir, in Cardoville's orgy, and in *The 120 Days*).
Why? Because at first sight sewing frustrates castration:
how can sewing (which is always: mend, make, repair) be
equivalent to: *mutilate, amputate, cut,* create an empty
space?

In fact, since the inversion of the sexes, or rather of
localities, rules the entire Sadian economy, this inversion
entails a reversal of castration: where *that* is, *it* must be removed; where *that* is not, in order to punish ejaculation
which remains triumphantly attached to this lack, there is
nothing for it but to punish it for being empty, to deny this
vacuum, not by filling it, but by closing it off, by sewing it.
Sewing is a secondary castration imposed in absence of the
penis: the most spiteful of castrations, indeed, since it makes
the body retrogress into the limbo of the sexless. To sew is
finally to remake a world without sewing, to return the
divinely cut-up body—whose cut-up state is the source
of all Sadian pleasure—to the abjection of the smooth
body, the total body.

The Red Thread

Metonymy is the sure path of horror: the instrument is
more terrible than the torture (whence the importance in
Sadian furnishing of those low tables upon which the accessories of torture *wait*). For sewing the victim, a "large
needle with thick red waxed thread" will be used. The more
extended the synecdoche, the more the instrument is broken
down into its tenuous elements (color, wax), the more the
horror grows and communicates itself (had we been told the
quality of the thread, it would have become intolerable);
here it is augmented by a kind of domestic tranquillity, the
tiny sewing material present in the instrument of torture.

The Head's Desire

In Sade, the males (fuckers, fuckees, lackeys, Hercules)
have a subordinate task: neither victims nor libertines, they

do not have access to language (they are mentioned infrequently, just for the sake of classification) and barely to a body (through the number of blows they give and the pints of sperm they produce): no mythology of virility. What makes the value of the sex is wit. Wit is both an *effervescence of the head* ("I see fucking coming out of his eyes") and a guarantee of capacity, for wit orders, invents, refines: " 'Oh,' I said to her, 'is it not true that the more wit one has the better one can enjoy the pleasures of vice?' "

Sadism

Sadism is only the coarse (vulgar) *contents* of the Sadian text.

The Principle of Tact

The Marquise de Sade, having asked the imprisoned Marquis to have his dirty linen sent out to her (knowing the Marquise, for what reason other than to have it washed?), Sade pretends to see in her request another, properly Sadian, motive: "Charming creature, you want my dirty linen, my old linen? Do you know, that is complete tact? you see how I sense the value of things. Listen, my angel, I have every wish in the world to satisfy you in this matter, because you know the respect I have for tastes, for fantasies: however baroque they may be, I find them all respectable, and because one is not the master of them, and because the most singular and bizarre of them, when well analyzed, always depends on a principle of tact."

Of course, Sade can be read as a plan of violence; however, he can also be read (and this is what he recommends us to do) *according to a principle of tact*. Sadian tact is not a class product, an attribute of civilization, a style of culture. It is a power of analysis and a means of ejaculation: analysis and ejaculation join together to produce an exaltation that is unknown in our societies and which constitutes therefore the most formidable of utopias. Violence follows a code worn out by millennia of human history; and to return violence is still to speak the same code. *The principle of tact* postulated by Sade can alone constitute, seeing that the bases of the Story will have changed, an absolutely new language, the unheard-of mutation, destined to subvert (not invert, but rather fragment, pluralize, pulverize) the very meaning of ejaculation.

LIVES

SADE

1. Etymological chain: *Sade, Sado, Sadone, Sazo, Sauza* (village of Saze). Again, lost in this lineage, the evil letter. In attaining the accursed name, brilliantly formulated (it has engendered a common noun), the letter that, as we say in French, *zebras,* fustigates, the *z,* has given way to the softest of dentals.

2. People living today in Saint-Germain-des-Prés must remember that they are living in a degenerate Sadian area. Sade was born in a room of the Hôtel de Condé, i.e., somewhere between the Rue Monsieur-le-Prince and the Rue de Condé; he was baptized in Saint-Sulpice; in 1777 he was arrested under a *lettre de cachet* at the Hôtel de Danemark, Rue Jacob (the very street where the French edition of this book is published), and from there brought to the prison dungeon at Vincennes.

3. In the spring of 1779, when Sade was imprisoned at Vincennes, he received a letter telling him that the orchard at La Coste was dazzling: cherry trees in bloom, apple trees, pear trees, hop bine, grapes, not to mention the burgeoning cypresses and oaks. For Sade, La Coste was a multiple, a total site; first, a Provençal site, the site of origin, of Return (throughout the first part of his life, Sade, although a fugitive, hunted, continued to *return* there, flouting prudence); next: an autarchic site, a miniature and total society over which he was the master, the unique source of his income, the site for study (his library was there), the site for theater

173

(they acted comedies), and the site for debauchery (Sade had servants, young peasant girls, young secretaries, brought in for séances at which the Marquise was also present). If, therefore, Sade kept returning to La Coste after his restless travels, it was not for the elevated purpose of purification in the countryside that impels the gangster in *The Asphalt Jungle* to return to die at the gate to the farm where he was born; as always, it had a plural, super-determined, probably contradictory meaning.

4. On Easter Sunday, 1768, at 9 A.M., on the Place des Victoires, accosting Rose Keller, a beggar (whom he was to whip several hours later in her house at Arcueil), the young Sade (twenty-eight years of age) was wearing a gray redingote, carrying a cane, a hunting knife—and a white muff. (Thus, at a time when the I.D. photograph was nonexistent, it is a paradox that the police report reveals the signifier in its description of the suspect's clothing: such as this delicious white muff, an article obviously donned to satisfy the *principle of tact* which seems always to have presided over the Marquis's sadistic activity—but not necessarily over that of sadists).

5. Sade likes theater costumes (forms which *make* the role); he wore them in his own daily life. When whipping Rose Keller, he disguises himself as a flogger (sleeveless vest over a naked torso; kerchief around the head as is worn by young Japanese cooks as they swiftly cut up live eels); later on, he prescribes for his wife the mourning costume she must wear for visiting a captive, unhappy husband: Dress as dark in color as possible, the bosom covered, "a large, very large bonnet without the hair it covers being dressed in any way, merely combed, a chignon, no braids."

6. *Household Sadism:* at Marseilles, Sade wants Marianne Lavergne to whip him with a parchment beater with bent pins which he takes from his pocket. The girl quails

before so exclusively functional an object (like a surgical instrument), and Sade orders the maidservant to bring a *heather broom;* this utensil is more familiar to Marianne and she has no hesitation in employing it to strike Sade across the buttocks.

7. The Lady President of Montreuil was objectively responsible for her son-in-law's persecutions during the entire first years of his life (perhaps she loved him? One day, someone told the Marquise that the Lady President "loved M. de Sade to distraction"). The impression we have of her character, however, is one of continual fear: fear of scandal, of "difficulties." Sade seems to have been a triumphant, troublesome victim; like a spoiled child, he is continually "teasing" (teasing is a sadistic passion) his respectable and conformist relations; wherever he goes, he provokes the terrified dismay of the guardians of order: everyone responsible for his confinement at the fort of Miolans (the King of Sardinia, the minister, the ambassador, the governor) is obsessed by the possibility of his escape—which does not fail to occur. The couple he forms with his persecutors is an aesthetic one: it is the malicious spectacle of a lively, elegant animal, both obsessed and inventive, mobile and tenacious, continually escaping and continually returning to the same area, while the giant mannequins, stiff, timorous, pompous, quite simply attempt to *contain* him (not *punish* him: this will only come later).

8. We need only read the Marquis's biography after having read his work to be convinced that he has put part of his work into his life—and not the opposite, as so-called literary science would have us believe. The "scandals" of Sade's life are not "models" of analogous situations drawn from his books. Real scenes and fantasized scenes are not directly related; all are no more than parallel duplications, more or less powerful (stronger in the work than in life), of a scene that is *absent, unfigured,* but not inarticulated,

whose site of infiguration and articulation can only be writing: Sade's work and his life traverse this writing area on an equal footing.

9. Returning to France from Italy, Sade has sent from Naples to La Coste two large cases; the second, weighing six quintals, travels on the boat *Aimable Marie;* it contains: "marbles, stones, a vase or amphora for storing Greek wines with resin, antique lamps, tear vases, all *à la* Greek and Roman, medals, idols, raw and worked stones from Vesuvius, a fine sepulchral urn intact, Etruscan vases, medals, a sculptured piece in serpentine, a bit of nitrate solfatara, seven sponges, a collection of shells, a tiny hermaphrodite and a vase of flowers . . . a marble dish decorated with singularly lifelike fruits of all varieties, chests of drawers of Vesuvian marble, a Saracen *buccherini* or cup, a Neapolitan knife, used clothing and prints . . . *Proofs of Religion,* a treatise on the existence of God . . . *The Rejected Tithe,* an almanac of plays, *The Gallant Saxon,* a military almanac, Mme de Pompadour's letters . . . a rhyming dictionary" (Lély, I, 568). This variety of wares is in every way worthy of Bouvard and Pécuchet: we lack only a few ellipses, a few asyndeta, to read here a bit of Flaubertian bravura. The Marquis, however, did not write this inventory; yet he is the one who amassed this collection, whose heteroclite cultural nature is derisory in relation to culture itself. Dual proof: of the baroque energy of which Sade was capable, and of the writing energy he put into his acts.

10. Sade had several young secretaries (Reillanne, young Malatié or Lamalatié, Rolland, Lefèvre, of whom he was jealous and whose portrait he pierced with a penknife), they are part of the Sadian game insofar as they are simultaneously servants for writing and for debauchery.

11. The list of Sade's detentions began in 1763 (he was twenty-three) and ended with his death in 1814. This almost uninterrupted imprisonment covers all the later years of the Ancien Régime, the revolutionary crisis and the Empire,

in short, it straddles the vast change accomplished by modern France. Whence it is easy to accuse, behind the various regimes that detained the Marquis, a higher entity, an unalterable source of repression (government or state) which encountered in Sade a symmetrical essence of Immorality and Subversion: Sade is like the exemplary hero of an eternal conflict: had they been less blind (but then, they were bourgeois, were they not?), Michelet and Hugo could have celebrated in him the fate of a martyr for liberty. Counter to this facile image, we must remember that Sade's detentions were *historical,* they derived their meaning from contemporary History, and since this History was precisely that of social change, there were in Sade's imprisonment at least two successive and different determinations and, to speak generically, two prisons. The first (Vincennes, the Bastille, until Sade's liberation by the dawning Revolution) was not a fact of Law. Although Sade had been judged and condemned to death by the Aix Parlement for sodomy (the Marseilles affair), although he was arrested in 1777 in the Rue Jacob after years of flight and more or less clandestine returns to La Coste, it was under the action of a *lettre de cachet* (issued by the king at the instigation of the Lady President of Montreuil); the accusation of sodomy lifted and the judgment overturned, he nonetheless went back to prison, since the *lettre de cachet,* independent of the court decree, continued in effect; and if he was liberated, it was because the Constituent Assembly abolished the *lettre de cachet* in 1790; thus it is easy to understand that Sade's first imprisonment had no penal or moral significance whatsoever; it was aimed essentially at preserving the honor of the Sade-Montreuil family from the Marquis's escapades; Sade was regarded as a libertine who was being "contained," and as a familial essence that was being saved; the context of this first imprisonment is a feudal one: the race commands, not morality; the king, dispenser of the *lettre de cachet,* is here merely the agent of the *people.* Sade's second imprisonment (from 1801 to his death: at Sainte-Pélagie, Bicêtre, and Charenton) is another matter; the Family has disappeared, the bourgeois State rules, it is this (and not a prudent mother-in-law) which has imprisoned Sade (although with no more of a trial than in the first instance) for having written his infamous books. There is a confusion (under which we are still laboring) established between morality and politics. This began with the Revolutionary Tribunal (whose always fatal sanction is familiar), which included as enemies of the people "individuals fostering moral depravity"; it continued in Jacobin discourse ("He brags," Sade's comrades in Piques said, "of having been shut up in the Bastille during the Ancien Régime so as to appear patriotic, whereas had he not been from the 'noble' caste, he would have been meted another kind of exemplary punishment"; in other words, bourgeois equality had *already*, retroactively, made him an immoral criminal); then in Republican discourse (*"Justine,"* a journalist said in 1799, "is a work as dangerous as the royalist newspaper *Le Nécessaire*, because if republics are founded on courage, they are upheld by morality; destruction of the latter always leads to the destruction of empires"); and finally, after Sade's death, in bourgeois discourse (Royer-Collard, Jules Janin, etc.). Sade's second prison (where he remains today, since his books are not freely sold in France) is no longer due to a family protecting itself, but to the apparatus of an entire State (justice, teaching, the press, criticism), which—in the Church's default—censors morality and controls literary production. Sade's first detention was segregative (cynical); the second was (is still) penal, moral; the first arose out of a practice, the second out of an ideology; this is proved by the fact that in imprisoning Sade the second time, it was necessary to mobilize a subject philosophy based totally on norm and deviation: for having written his books, Sade was shut up as a madman.

12. In certain of the letters he received or wrote at Vincennes or in the Bastille, Sade discerned or inserted number utterances which he called *signals*. These signals helped him to imagine or even to read (supposing they were put there intentionally by his correspondent and had escaped the censor) the number of days between receipt and a visit from his wife, an authorization for outdoor recreation, or his freedom; these signals are for the most part malevolent ("The number system is working against me . . ."). The mania for numbers can be read at various levels; first, neurotic defense: in his fiction, Sade is constantly bookkeeping: classes of subjects, orgasms, victims, and, above all, like Ignatius Loyola, in a purely obsessive twist, he accounts for his own oversights, his errors in numbering; further, number, when it deranges a rational system (we may rather say made purposely to derange it), has the power to produce a surrealistic shock: "On the 18th at 9, the clock chimed 26 times," Sade notes in his Journal; finally, number is the triumphant path of access to the signifier (here as a pun involving the similarity of pronunciation, in French, of the past tense of "to come," *vint,* and the number "twenty," *vingt*): ("The other day, because we needed a 24, a flunkey pretending to be M. le Noir [a police officer], and so that I might write to Monsieur Le Noir, *came* at 4 (*vint le 4*), thus 24 (*vingt-quatre*)." Numeration is the beginning of writing, its liberating positioning: a connection apparently censured in the history of ideography, if we are to believe J.-L. Schefer's current work on hieroglyphics and cuneiform: the phonological theory of language (Jakobson) unduly separates the linguist from writing; calculation will bring him closer.

13. Sade had a phobia: the sea. What will be given schoolchildren to read: Baudelaire's poem ("Free man, you will always cherish the sea . . .") or Sade's avowal ("I've always feared and immensely disliked the sea . . .")?

14. One of Sade's principal persecutors, Police Lieu-

tenant Sartine, suffered from a psychopathological condition which in a *just* (equal) society would have entailed his imprisonment on the same footing as his victim: he was a wig fetishist: "His library contained all kinds of wigs of all sizes: he put them on according to the circumstances; among others, he owned a good-luck wig (with five loosely hanging little curls) and a wig for interrogating criminals, a kind of snake headdress called the *inexorable*" (Lély, II, 90). Aware of the phallic value of the braid, we can imagine how Sade must have longed to clip the toupees of his hated cop.

15. In the social game of his time, doubly complicated because—rare in history—it was both synchronic and diachronic, displaying the (apparently immobile) *tableau* of classes under the Ancien Régime and class changes (under the Revolution), Sade was extremely mobile: a social *joker,* able to occupy any niche in the class system; Lord of La Coste, he was supplanted in Mlle Colet's affections by a bourgeois, a collector of rents, who presented the actress with a magnificent *sultan* (a dressing table); later, a member of the Piques sector, he assumes the socially neutral figure of a man of letters, a dramatist; struck from the list of émigrés and owing to a confusion of first names that exists today, he was able (or at least his family was) to appear as he wished according to the varied moments of History on this turnstile of social class. He honors the sociological notion of social *mobility,* but in a ludic sense; he moves up and down on the social scale like a bottle imp; a reflection, once again in the socio-economic meaning of the term, he makes this reflection not the imitation or product of a determination, but the unselfconscious *game* of a mirror. In this carrousel of roles, one fixed point: manners, way of life, which were always aristocratic.

16. Sade was very fond of dogs, spaniels, and setters; he had them at Miolans, asked for them at Vincennes. Through what moral (or worse: virile) law should the greatest of subversions exclude minor affection, that for animals?

17. At Vincennes in 1783, the penitentiary administration forbade the prisoner's receiving Rousseau's *Confessions*. Sade comments: "They honor me in thinking that a deist author could be a bad book for me; I wish I were at that point. . . . Understand, it is the point one is at that makes a thing good or bad, and not the thing itself. . . . Start there, dear sirs, and by sending me the book I request, be sensible enough to understand that for died-in-the-wool bigots like yourselves, Rousseau can be a dangerous author, and that makes it an excellent book for me. For me, Jean-Jacques is what the *Imitation of Christ* is for you. . . ." Censorship is abhorrent on two levels: because it is repressive, because it is stupid; so that we always have the contradictory urge to combat it and to teach it a lesson.

18. Suddenly transferred from Vincennes to the Bastille, Sade made a great fuss because he had not been allowed to bring his *big pillow,* without which he was unable to sleep, since he slept with his head unusually high: "The barbarians!".

19. Throughout his life, the Marquis de Sade's passion was not erotic (eroticism is very different from passion); it was theatrical: youthful liaisons with several young ladies of the Opéra, engaging the actor Bourdais to play for six months at La Coste, and in his torment, one idea: to have his plays performed; barely out of prison (1790), repeated requests to the actors of the Comédie Française; and finally, of course, theater at Charenton.

20. A plurality of which Sade was well aware, since he laughs at it: in 1793, Citizen Sade was proposed as a juror in a common-law case (a matter of forged promissory notes): the dual hearing of the Sadian text (of which Sade's life is a part): the apologist of crime and its judge are united in the same subject, as the Saussurian anagram is inscribed in a Vedic verse (but what remains of a subject that subjects itself with alacrity to a dual inscription?).

21. *Corridor Philosophy:* Imprisoned at Sainte-Pélagie

(at sixty-three years of age), Sade, we are told, used "every means his imagination could suggest . . . to seduce and corrupt the young people (to slake his lubricity with young fools) who were imprisoned in Sainte-Pélagie owing to unfortunate circumstances and put by chance in the same corridor as himself."

22. Any detention is a system: a bitter struggle exists within this system, not to get free of it (this was beyond Sade's power), but to break through its constraints. A prisoner for some twenty-five years of his life, Sade in prison had two fixations: outdoor exercise and writing, which governors and ministers were continually allowing and taking away from him like a rattle from a baby. The need and the desire for outdoor exercise are easily understood (although Sade always linked its privation to a symbolic theme, obesity). The repression, obviously, as anyone can see, of writing is as good as censoring the book; what is poignant here, however, is that writing is forbidden in its *physical* form; Sade was denied "any use of pencil, ink, pen, and paper." Censored are hand, muscle, blood. Castration is circumscribed, the scriptural sperm can no longer flow; detention becomes retention; without exercise, without a pen, Sade becomes *bloated,* becomes a eunuch.

FOURIER

1. Fourier: a *shop steward* ("A shop steward who will refute political and moral libraries, the shameful fruit of ancient and modern quackeries"). At Besançon, his parents ran a cloth and spice store: *trade,* execrated, *spice,* adored

183 | *Lives*

in the form of a *body,* the aromale which (among other things) will perfume the seas; at the court of the King of Morocco, there is said to be a Director of the Royal Scents: aside from the monarchy, and the director, Fourier would have been enchanted by this title.

2. Fourier was contemporary with the two greatest events of Modern History: the Revolution and the Empire. Yet in this social philosopher's work, no trace of these two cataclysms; Napoleon is merely the person who wanted to control interior transport, *rolling stock,* which is a material Transition (political Transition is *brokerage*).

3. Fourier's enchantments: The City and its gardens, the pleasures of the Palais-Royal. In his work there is a dream of the *brilliant:* sensual brilliance, the brilliance of food and of love: this brilliance that is already to be found, in a play on words, in the name of his brother-in-law, in whose company he traveled and probably discovered the *mirlitons* (little spiced cakes) of Paris: Brillat-Savarin.

4. Fourier hated old cities: Rouen.

5. At Lyons, Fourier learned trade: he was ruined by the shipwreck of a boat at Leghorn (maritime trade in Harmony: cargoes of rainets and lemons, the barter of wheat and sugar).

6. Fourier survived the Terror "only at the cost of repeated lies"; on the other hand, he praised Napoleon "in order to conform to the customs of 1808, which demanded that every work emit a puff of incense for the Emperor."

7. Inter-Text: Claude de Saint-Martin, Sénancour, Restif de la Bretonne, Diderot, Rousseau, Kepler, Newton.

8. Fourier experienced *reversals:* ruined, he took subordinate employments, interspersed with living by his wits; a writer, he lived off others, and was put up for long periods of time by his family and friends in Bugey and in the Jura.

9. His knowledge: mathematical and experimental sciences, music, geography, astronomy.

10. His old age: he surrounded himself with cats and flowers.

11. His concierge found him dead in his dressing gown, kneeling among the flowerpots.

12. Fourier had read Sade.